DAR

DARE TO RISK

8 sessions on the challenges of risk-taking

by Arlene R. Inouye

VICTOR BOOKS
A DIVISION OF SCRIPTURE PRESS PUBLICATIONS INC.
USA CANADA ENGLAND

Most Scripture quotations are taken from the *Holy Bible, New International Version*®. Copyright © 1973, 1978, 1984 by International Bible Society. Used by permission of Zondervan Publishing House. All rights reserved. Other quotations are from the *New Revised Standard Version Bible* (NRSV), © 1989, Thomas Nelson, Inc. Used by permission of the National Council of the Churches of Christ in the United States of America.

Copyediting: Jane Vogel
Cover Design: Joe DeLeon
Cover Illustration: Richard McNeel
Interior Illustrations: Al Hering

Recommended Dewey Decimal Classification: 301.402
Suggested Subject Heading: SMALL GROUPS: RISK-TAKING

Library of Congress Catalog Card Number: 92-26638
ISBN: 1-56476-024-3

1 2 3 4 5 6 7 8 9 10 Printing / Year 96 95 94 93 92

© 1992 by SP Publications, Inc. All rights reserved. Printed in the United States of America. No part of this book may be reproduced without written permission, except for brief quotations in books, critical articles, and reviews.

VICTOR BOOKS
A division of SP Publications, Inc.
          Wheaton, Illinois 60187

CONTENTS

PURPOSE: To gain the insight, support, and experience needed to take risks in faith and obedience to God.

INTRODUCTION	7
IS THIS YOUR FIRST SMALL GROUP?	9

SESSION 1—THE CHALLENGE OF RISK-TAKING   13
Are you willing to take the risks?

SESSION 2—PETER'S "OUT-OF-THE-BOAT" EXPERIENCE   19
What prevents you from taking risks?

SESSION 3—GETTING OUT OF THE BOAT WITH OUR MATERIAL NEEDS   25
How do your possessions get in the way of your obedience to God?

SESSION 4—GETTING OUT OF THE BOAT WITH OUR CAREERS   33
Are you willing to risk your career to follow Jesus?

SESSION 5—GETTING OUT OF THE BOAT WITH OUR RELATIONSHIPS   39
Which of your relationships are at risk if you respond to Jesus?

SESSION 6—GETTING OUT OF THE BOAT WITH OUR CONVICTIONS   47
How is God asking you to step out of your comfort zone to live out your convictions?

SESSION 7—STAYING AFLOAT WITH GOD   55
Are you keeping fellowship with God?

SESSION 8—STAYING AFLOAT WITH THE COMMUNITY OF FAITH   63
How can you support one another in your risk-taking?

DEAR SMALL GROUP LEADER   71
LEADER'S GUIDE   73

INTRODUCTION

Dare to Risk is for people who want to know more about how to live out their commitment to Christ. An in-depth Leader's Guide is included at the back of the book with suggested time guidelines to help you structure your emphases. Each of the 8 sessions contains the following elements:

❑ **GroupSpeak**—quotes from group members that capsulize what the session is about.

❑ **Getting Acquainted**—activities or selected readings to help you begin thinking and sharing from your life and experiences about the subject of the session. Use only those options that seem appropriate for your group.

❑ **Gaining Insight**—questions and in-depth Bible study help you gain principles from Scripture for life-related application.

❑ **Growing By Doing**—an opportunity to practice the Truth learned in the Gaining Insight section.

❑ **Going The Second Mile**—a personal enrichment section for you to do on your own.

❑ **Growing As A Leader**—an additional section in the Leader's Guide for the development and assessment of leadership skills.

❑ **Pocket Principles**—brief guidelines inserted in the Leader's Guide to help the Group Leader learn small group leadership skills as needed.

❑ **Session Objectives**—goals listed in the Leader's Guide that describe what should happen in the group by the end of the session.

IS THIS YOUR FIRST SMALL GROUP?

'smol grüp: A limited number of individuals assembled together having some unifying relationship.

**Kris'chen
'smol grüp:** 4–12 persons who meet together on a regular basis, over a determined period of time, for the shared purpose of pursuing biblical truth. They seek to mature in Christ and become equipped to serve as His ministers in the world.

Picture Your First Small Group.

List some words that describe what you want your small group to look like.

What Kind Of Small Group Do You Have?
People form all kinds of groups based on gender, age, marital status, and so forth. There are advantages and disadvantages to each. Here are just a few:

❑ **Same Age Groups** will probably share similar needs and interests.

Intergenerational Groups bring together people with different perspectives and life experiences.

❏ **Men's or Women's Groups** usually allow greater freedom in sharing and deal with more focused topics.

❏ **Singles or Married Groups** determine their relationship emphases based on the needs of a particular marital status.

❏ **Mixed Gender Groups (singles and/or couples)** stimulate interaction and broaden viewpoints while reflecting varied lifestyles.

However, the most important area of "alikeness" to consider when forming a group is an **agreed-on purpose.** Differences in purpose will sabotage your group and keep its members from bonding. If, for example, Mark wants to pray but not play while Jan's goal is to learn through playing, then Mark and Jan's group will probably not go anywhere. People need different groups at different times in their lives. Some groups will focus on sharing and accountability, some on work projects or service, and others on worship. *Your small group must be made up of persons who have similar goals.*

How Big Should Your Small Group Be?

The **fewest** people to include would be **4**. Accountability will be high, but absenteeism may become a problem.

The **most** to include would be **12**. But you will need to subdivide regularly into groups of 3 or 4 if you want people to feel cared for and to have time for sharing.

How Long Should You Meet?

8 Weeks gives you a start toward becoming a close community, but doesn't overburden busy schedules. Count on needing three or four weeks to develop a significant trust level. The smaller the group, the more quickly trust develops.

Weekly Meetings will establish bonding at a good pace and allow for accountability. The least you can meet and still be an effective group is once a month. If you choose the latter, work at individual contact among group members between meetings.

You will need **75 minutes** to accomplish a quality meeting. The larger the size, the more time it takes to become a healthy group. Serving refreshments will add 20–30 minutes, and singing and/or prayer time, another 20–30 minutes. Your time duration may be determined by the time of day you meet and by the amount of energy members bring to the group. Better to start small and ask for more time when it is needed because of growth.

What Will Your Group Do?

To be effective, each small group meeting should include:

1. Sharing—You need to share who you are and what is happening in your life. This serves as a basis for relationship building and becomes a springboard for searching out scriptural truth.

2. Scripture—There must always be biblical input from the Lord to teach, rebuke, correct, and train in right living. Such material serves to move your group in the direction of maturity in Christ and protects from pooled ignorance and distorted introspection.

3. Truth in practice—It is vital to provide opportunities for *doing* the Word of God. Experiencing this within the group insures greater likelihood that insights gained will be utilized in everyday living.

Other elements your group may wish to add to these three are: a time of **worship, specific prayer** for group members, **shared projects**, a time to **socialize** and enjoy **refreshments**, and **recreation**.

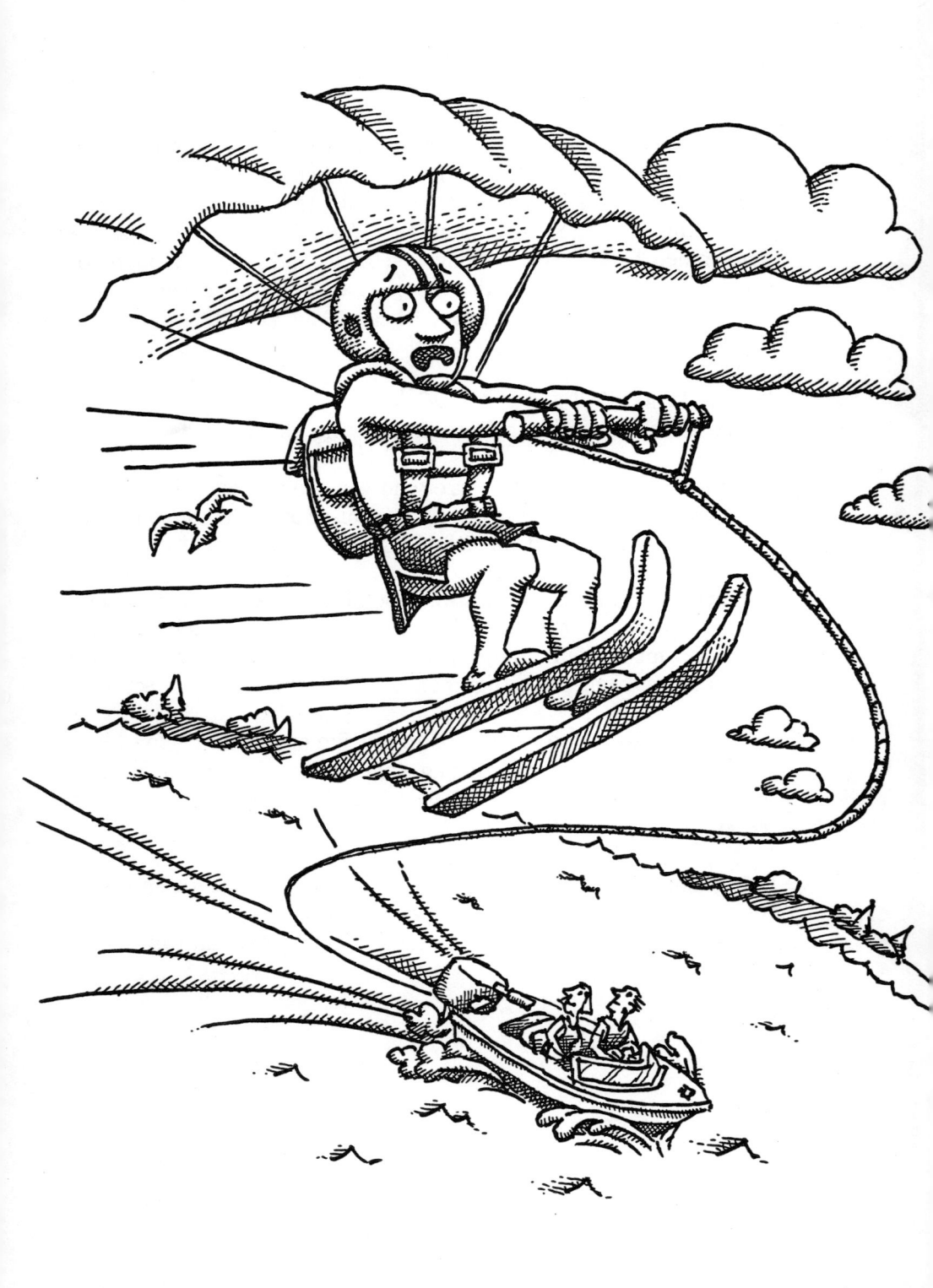

ONE

The Challenge of Risk-taking

GroupSpeak: *"I know that as Christians we're supposed to obey God, whatever the cost, but that kind of obedience is really hard. It means moving out of my comfort zone and involves risks I'm not sure I can take...."*

Comfort Zone or Twilight Zone?
Much of risk-taking means moving out of our comfort zones. It often appears hazardous to our health. When God asks us to do something that seems too difficult for us, we may want to resist or refuse to obey. The familiar is much easier.

Dare to Risk is meant to help us to understand what it means to live by faith in obedience to God, even when that requires taking risks. We'll examine certain areas of our personal lives and see whether God is asking us to leave what's familiar to do something different or to enter the unknown. We will use the example of Peter and his walk on water as a framework to understand risk-taking in the Christian life. During the eight sessions together, we will encourage one another to leave our comfort zones and enter new "zones" with faith and courage.

Each of us responds to risk-taking differently. Some of us take many risks. Others of us are a lot more cautious. As a

DARE TO RISK

way to get to know each other better in our first meeting together, let's find out about each other's risk-taking behavior.

GETTING ACQUAINTED

Risky or Risk-free?
As a way to get to know each other and assess your own risk-taking behavior, check the boxes that most reflect your responses to the following:

1. When I go to a restaurant I tend to . . .
   ❑ Order the usual.
   ❑ Try something new.

2. When I grocery shop, I tend to . . .
   ❑ Stick to name brands.
   ❑ Try the newest products.

3. When it comes to volunteering, I'll . . .
   ❑ Offer to do something I haven't done before.
   ❑ Do something only if I have experience with it.

4. When it comes to life in general, I tend to . . .
   ❑ Leap before I look.
   ❑ Look before I leap.
   ❑ Look and not leap.

5. My life as a disciple tends to be life in . . .
   ❑ A comfort zone (familiar).
   ❑ A twilight zone (unknown).

6. I feel like my participation in this group is . . .
   ❑ Risk-free.
   ❑ A little risky for me.
   ❑ Fairly risky for me.
   ❑ Very risky for me.

After answering these questions, spend time as a group to share your responses. Notice similarities and differences among you. How do your personalities reflect differences in your risk-taking behavior?

THE CHALLENGE OF RISK-TAKING

GAINING INSIGHT

Real-life Risk

We encounter risks to varying degrees every day. *Webster's Dictionary* defines risk as the possibility of loss or injury. When people take risks they expose themselves to potential hazard or danger. The danger may or may not be real, but it is certainly felt. And it naturally creates fear and anxiety for most of us.

Write down here one risk, big or small, you took recently. What was the outcome?

Scripture Study

The Bible has some things to say about risk-taking. The story of Peter's walking on the water (Matthew 14:22-33) is one example. Let's look at this story by role-playing as a group, noting how the different characters responded to the circumstances.

NARRATOR: **²²Immediately Jesus made the disciples get into the boat and go on ahead of Him to the other side, while He dismissed the crowd. ²³After He had dismissed them, He went up on a mountainside by Himself to pray. When evening came, He was there alone, ²⁴but the boat was already a considerable distance from land, buffeted by the waves because the wind was against it. ²⁵During the fourth watch of the night Jesus went out to them, walking on the lake. ²⁶When the disciples saw Him walking on the lake, they were terrified.**

DISCIPLES: **It's a ghost!**

NARRATOR: **They said, and cried out in fear. ²⁷But Jesus immediately said to them:**

JESUS: **Take courage! It is I. Don't be afraid.**

PETER: **²⁸Lord, if it's You, tell me to come to You on the water.**

DARE TO RISK

JESUS: ²⁹**Come.**

NARRATOR: **Then Peter got down out of the boat, walked on the water and came toward Jesus. ³⁰But when he saw the wind, he was afraid and, beginning to sink, cried out,**

PETER: **Lord, save me!**

NARRATOR: **³¹Immediately Jesus reached out His hand and caught him.**

JESUS: **You of little faith, why did you doubt?**

NARRATOR: **³²And when they climbed into the boat, the wind died down. ³³Then those who were in the boat worshiped Him, saying,**

DISCIPLES: **Truly You are the Son of God.**

❏ What did you notice or learn about the disciples in the story?

❏ What did you notice or learn about Peter?

❏ What did you notice or learn about Jesus?

❏ As you look at this passage, what is God saying to you about your own risk-taking behavior?

GROWING BY DOING

Making Connections

In role-playing the story, your part may or may not have represented the person you could identify with the best.

THE CHALLENGE OF RISK-TAKING

Take a few minutes to reread the Bible passage and ask yourself:
- Who do I see myself as? Which person do I understand or identify with the most?
- Why do I identify with this person?
- Who in the passage would I like to be more like? Why?
- What could I do this week to become more like that person?

After reflecting on these questions, share your responses with one other person in your group. Then pray for one another and what God wants to teach you through this study on risk-taking.

GOING THE SECOND MILE

During the week, try to keep in mind what you have experienced this first meeting. Take special note of how you respond to any risks that come your way. Is your behavior any different from your usual response as a result of what you experienced in session 1? Come prepared to share your thoughts, feelings, and experiences next time.

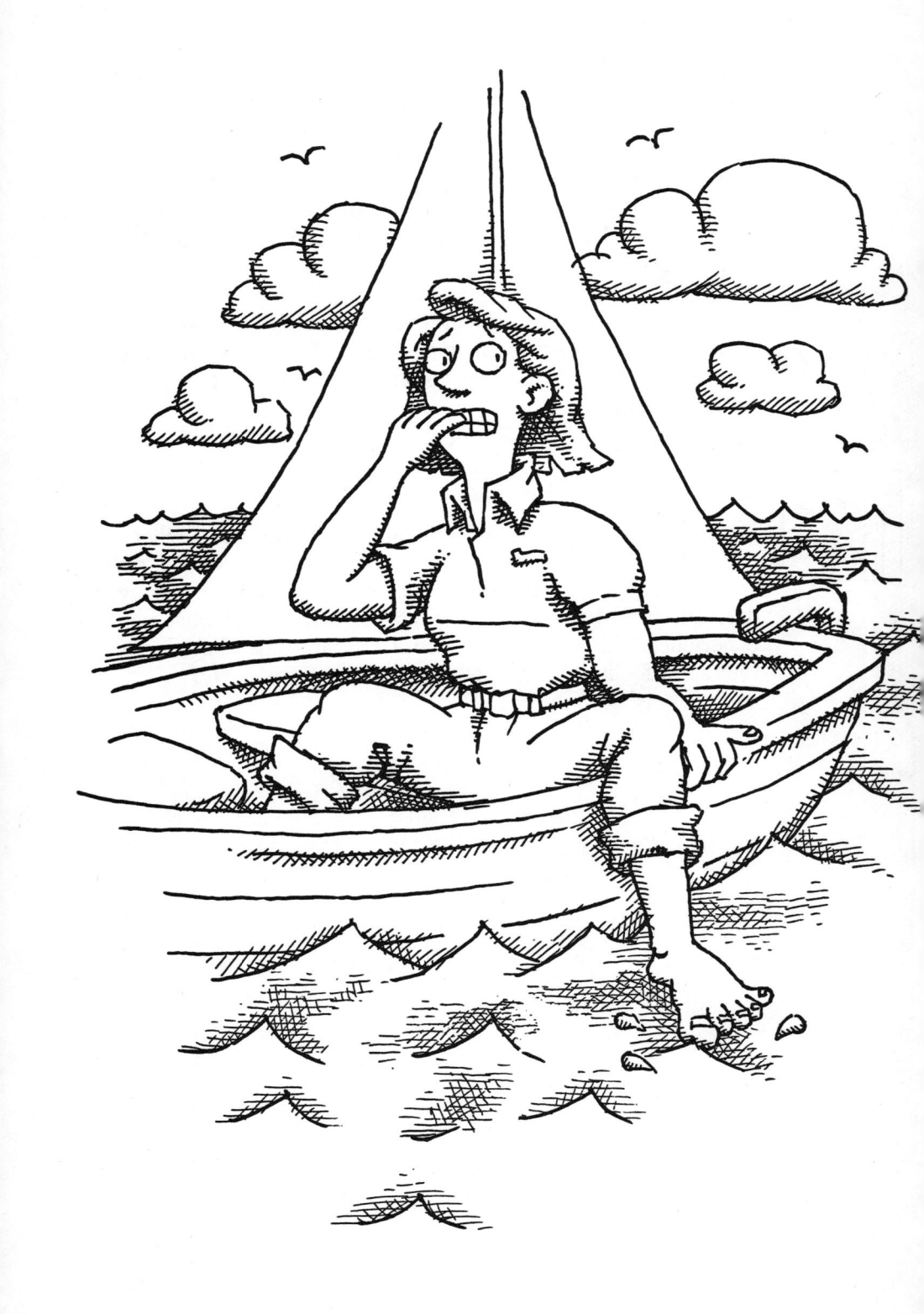

TWO

Peter's "Out-of-the-Boat" Experience

GroupSpeak: *"I know that sometimes God asks us to do things that feel risky to us. The problem is that along with hearing His voice I hear a lot of other voices that try to stop me from obeying Him. These voices tell me, 'I'll fail,' 'I'm inadequate,' 'I'll look foolish,' or, 'I'm not capable.' And I end up feeling like I don't have enough faith to trust Him."*

Developing Trust

The Apostle Paul tells us that we are to live by faith and not by sight (2 Corinthians 5:7). This is hard for most of us to do because we like to look where we're going. We like to have control of our lives. Unknowns scare us. Choosing to take risks means that we must exercise faith. We have to believe that, even though we're not sure about the outcome of our obedience, God is trustworthy.

Peter deepened his trust through his experience with Jesus on the Sea of Galilee. When Jesus commanded Peter to come to Him on the water, Peter had to choose to get out of the boat and walk on water. He had to trust that, if he obeyed, Jesus would not let him sink. And He didn't. What a lesson of good news to all of us!

DARE TO RISK

GETTING ACQUAINTED
Walking by Faith
One of the ways we learn to trust God is by experiencing the trustworthiness of others. To experience this in our group, the group leader will give instructions for a "faith walk." After the activity, reflect on your experience of being blindfolded or watching some of your group members that way. Then respond to these questions in your group:

❏ What was it like (or what do you think it was like) not being able to see and having to rely on others to guide you?

❏ What, if anything, hindered you from trusting your guide?

❏ What hinders you personally from trusting God completely?

GAINING INSIGHT
A Man Called Peter
Read aloud Matthew 14:22-33. As you do, think about the person of Peter.

²²Immediately Jesus made the disciples get into the boat and go on ahead of Him to the other side, while He dismissed the crowd. ²³After He had dismissed them, He went up on a mountainside by Himself to pray. When evening came, He was there alone, ²⁴but the boat was already a considerable distance from land, buffeted by the waves because the wind was against it.

²⁵During the fourth watch of the night Jesus went out to them, walking on the lake. ²⁶When the disciples saw Him walking on the lake, they were terrified. "It's a ghost," they said, and cried out in fear.

²⁷But Jesus immediately said to them: "Take courage! It is I. Don't be afraid."

²⁸"Lord, if it's You," Peter replied, "tell me to come to You on the water."

20

PETER'S "OUT-OF-THE-BOAT" EXPERIENCE

²⁹**"Come," He said. Then Peter got down out of the boat, walked on the water and came toward Jesus. ³⁰But when he saw the wind, he was afraid and, beginning to sink, cried out, "Lord, save me!"**

³¹**Immediately Jesus reached out His hand and caught him. "You of little faith," He said, "why did you doubt?"**

³²**And when they climbed into the boat, the wind died down. ³³Then those who were in the boat worshiped Him, saying, "Truly You are the Son of God."**

Matthew 14:22-33

In the Gospel accounts, Peter is portrayed as impetuous and impulsive. He's the type who leaps before he looks. He's a risk-taker. Yet Peter is the one on whom Jesus chose to build His church.

In our passage, we see the disciples tossed about by a violent storm. They're terrified, but when Jesus identifies Himself, Peter responds by saying, "Lord, if it's You, tell me to come to You on the water."

❏ What do you think Peter's motives were when he made this statement?

Even though we can't be sure of Peter's motives, Jesus responded to Peter's initiative. Jesus told him, "Come!" And once Jesus commanded Peter to come, it became an issue of obedience. Once it became clear to Peter what Jesus was asking of him, he had to choose to stay in the boat or get out of it, to obey or not to obey.

❏ When have you encountered a situation or circumstance where you heard Jesus say, "Come!" and you had to decide to obey or not to obey?

Like Peter, we may choose to get out of the boat and move out of our comfort zone, but then get distracted by the winds and waves in life.

❑ What are some winds and waves that come to people, and which of these have you experienced personally?

The distractions caused Peter to take his eyes off Jesus, and that's when he started to sink. But Peter knew who to turn to as he began to drown. He didn't simply cry out, "Somebody, save me!" Rather, he cried out, "Lord, save me!" And notice too that Jesus saved Peter even though he doubted and got distracted.

❑ If you were to interview Peter, how do you think he would respond to this question: "What lessons did you learn about Jesus and being obedient in risk-taking?"

Peter's risk-taking strengthened his faith. He got to do the seemingly impossible and experience life with Jesus in a way the others in the boat had not. But that wasn't all. The rest of the disciples learned and grew too.

❑ What effect do you think Peter's risk-taking had on the lives of others?

The experience of Peter's walk on water tells us that when the Lord asks us to do the seemingly impossible and we obey, we discover firsthand that with God all things are possible. When things are out of our hands, we can then most clearly see the hand of God. When we are without power of our own, the power of God comes to us. The power which raised Jesus from the dead is the very same power God uses to keep secure all those who believe in Him. It is the power that calms the storms in our lives and enables us to be obedient and experience peace in the midst of turmoil.

God desires Peter's story to be our own. In whatever ways the Lord asks us to take risks in obedience and faith, we can

PETER'S "OUT-OF-THE-BOAT" EXPERIENCE

dare to risk because He assures us: The One who calls us out of the boat has the power to keep us afloat.

GROWING BY DOING

Since God desires Peter's story to be our own, we need to personalize it. The following questions are intended to help us do that. Share your responses with the others.

- ❏ Where in your life right now do you need to hear Jesus say to you, "Take courage! It is I. Don't be afraid"?
- ❏ Where in your life are you hearing Jesus say, "Come!" and what does it involve?
- ❏ Where in your life do you need to cry out, "Lord, save me"?

GOING THE SECOND MILE

Participating in a discussion is a helpful way to learn. We can build on what we have learned in discussion when we write down our thoughts or responses to specific questions. It helps us to better internalize biblical truth. During the week, try journaling your thoughts as you again think about the questions in Growing by Doing. As you seek to apply to your own life Jesus' words, "Take courage" and "Come!" and discern where you need to tell Jesus, "Save me!" allow what you put on paper to inform your prayers.

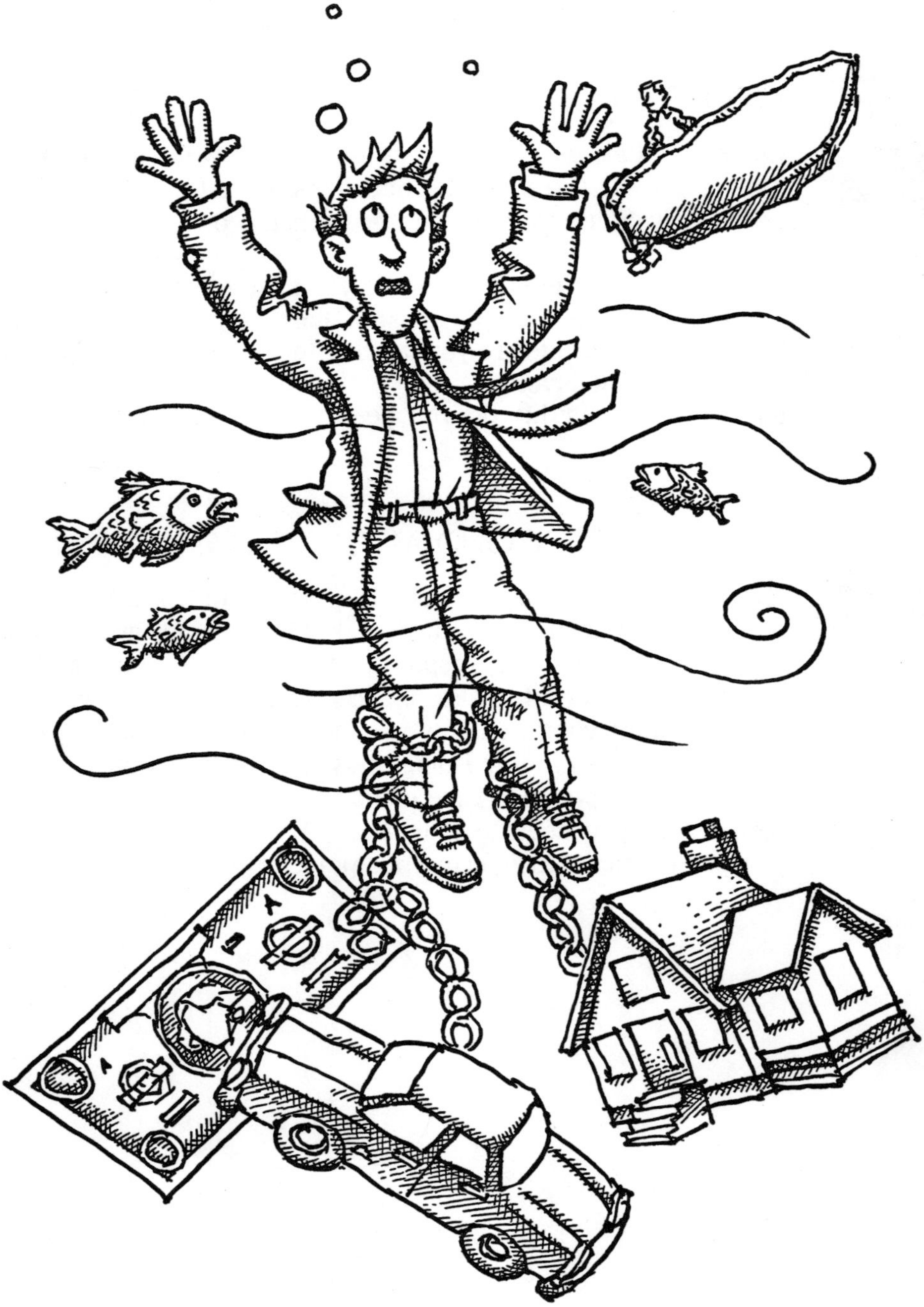

THREE

Getting Out of the Boat with Our Material Needs

Have you ever felt:

GroupSpeak: *"If only I had more money, life would be so much easier. I wouldn't have to worry about finances or making ends meet. I'd be freed up to enjoy life more, buy the things I want, and help others less fortunate than I am."*

Possessions

"If I were a rich man...." So goes the line from one of the famous songs sung in the musical "Fiddler on the Roof." At one time or another, all of us have probably wanted more money or possessions than we have had. We engage in wishful thinking: "If only I were rich," "If only I had more money," "If only...."

Read Matt 19:21-22

Jesus also used "if" statements. One of them is recorded in the Gospel of Matthew. It occurs in a conversation that Jesus had with a rich young man: "If you want to be perfect, go, sell your possessions and give to the poor, and you will have treasure in heaven. Then come, follow Me" (19:21). We're told that the man, on hearing these words, went away sad, for he had many possessions. *and anxious*

25

DARE TO RISK

Many of us can identify with the young man, not because we are rich or have so many possessions, but because we find it hard to trust God for our material needs and not to overvalue the things we do have. Yet this is a big part of what it means to be a disciple of Jesus. And it's easier said than done! How can we help each other exercise more faith and obedience in the area of our material needs and possessions?

GETTING ACQUAINTED

Anxiety Levels

On a scale from 0 to 10, with 0 being no anxiety whatsoever and 10 being overly anxious, rate yourself given these situations:

1. You learn that there's not enough money for the rent or mortage. ___
2. A good friend no longer has a car and asks if she can borrow your car twice a week to do business and errands. ___
3. Your pastor gives a sermon on how Christians should tithe at least 10 percent of their gross income to the church. ___
4. You have just lost your job. ___
5. You have been unemployed for six months and your savings account is nearly depleted. ___
6. You've been unemployed for six months, your savings account is nearly depleted, and you're told that you should still tithe to the church. ___
7. Someone in your small group expresses a financial need. You have the ability to meet the need if you use the money you set aside for your future emergencies. ___
8. Your house just burned down. You lost all your possessions. ___
9. You feel called to quit your job and go into full-time Christian work, but your income will not be enough to support your family. ___
10. Your neighbor borrowed your microwave oven for a party and accidentally broke it. He has no money to repair it. ___

TOTAL divided by 10 ___

GETTING OUT OF THE BOAT WITH OUR MATERIAL NEEDS

Add up the numbers you marked, divide the total by 10, and put the final figure in the bottom space. What does this figure reveal about your anxiety levels with reference to trusting God with your material needs and possessions? (3.4)

Necessity or Luxury? *don't do*
Categorize the following according to whether or not you think the item is a necessity or luxury to you, and also mark if you possess it:

	NECESSITY	LUXURY	I POSSESS
1. House/Condo/Apt.	___	___	___
2. Car	___	___	___
3. Food	___	___	___
4. Microwave oven	___	___	___
5. Dishwasher	___	___	___
6. Washer and dryer	___	___	___
7. Clothing	___	___	___
8. Computer	___	___	___
9. Television	___	___	___
10. Books	___	___	___
11. VCR	___	___	___
12. Stereo equipment	___	___	___
13. Toiletries	___	___	___
14. Telephone	___	___	___
TOTAL:	___	___	___

GAINING INSIGHT

A Choice and a Promise

Have some one read this!!

Read aloud Matthew 6:24-34.
24"No one can serve two masters. Either he will hate the one and love the other, or he will be devoted to the one and despise the other. You cannot serve both God and Money.

25Therefore I tell you, do not worry about your life, what you will eat or drink; or about your body, what you will wear. Is

27

not life more important than food, and the body more important than clothes? ²⁶Look at the birds of the air; they do not sow or reap or store away in barns, and yet your heavenly Father feeds them. Are you not much more valuable than they? ²⁷Who of you by worrying can add a single hour to his life?

²⁸And why do you worry about clothes? See how the lilies of the field grow. They do not labor or spin. ²⁹Yet I tell you that not even Solomon in all his splendor was dressed like one of these. ³⁰If that is how God clothes the grass of the field, which is here today and tomorrow is thrown into the fire, will He not much more clothe you, O you of little faith? ³¹So do not worry, saying, "What shall we eat?" or "What shall we drink?" or "What shall we wear?" ³²For the pagans run after all these things, and your heavenly Father knows that you need them. ³³But seek first His kingdom and His righteousness, and all these things will be given to you as well. ³⁴Therefore do not worry about tomorrow, for tomorrow will worry about itself. Each day has enough trouble of its own.

Matthew 6:24-34

☐ What do you think Jesus meant when He said, "You cannot serve God and Money"? (v. 25) *And which one do you serve?*

Jesus seems to be saying that there is no "middle of the road." We can't "have our cake and eat it too." As David Watson, author of *Called and Committed,* writes, "Most of us would like to find some happy compromise. Of course we want to seek first the kingdom of God; but earthly treasures continue to attract us, cause us anxiety and erode our faith. Wanting the best of both worlds, we lose the transforming power of the kingdom of God" (pp. 164–65).

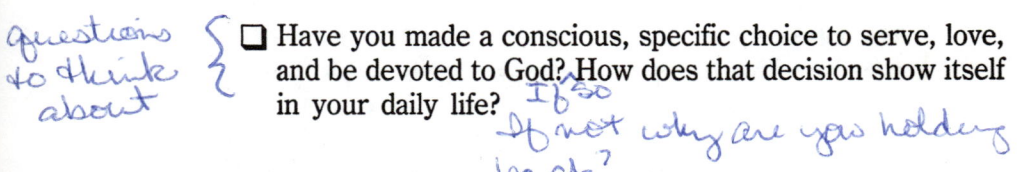

questions to think about

☐ Have you made a conscious, specific choice to serve, love, and be devoted to God? How does that decision show itself in your daily life? *If so. If not why are you holding back?*

GETTING OUT OF THE BOAT WITH OUR MATERIAL NEEDS

In verses 25-34, Jesus speaks specifically about anxiety, a mental state of being overly concerned and worried. He cites how the birds and the lilies are taken care of by God, and how humans are much more important to Him. However, Jesus is not saying that, since the birds and lilies do not work for their food or existence, neither should we. Rather, Jesus' point is that all creatures' needs are met by the Heavenly Father. When we as children of God know and live out this truth, we experience freedom from anxiety.

Most of us know what it's like to be stressed out about finances and making ends meet. We also know that such negative feelings are not very helpful or productive. Jesus says that worrying can't add a single hour to our span of life (v. 27). — *it doesn't stop here either — some people are not negative but they that's where it ends we must then do something to help*

☐ Right now, what hinders you from wholeheartedly trusting God to meet all your material needs? *Or what are somethings that hinder people in general?*

At moment is right ask these ?'s

☐ Right now, what hinders you from letting go of and trusting God with your material possessions?

☐ *Is it bad to want or dream about what you want in the future — Matt 7:7-8 ask God for what* *especially "seek and you will find"*

Jesus does not simply state that His followers are not to be anxious. Instead, he tells us to do something positive and action-oriented: "Seek first His kingdom and His righteousness..." (v. 33).

☑ What do you think it means to seek first the kingdom of God and His righteousness?

If you are a christian and are truly seeking God's will it okay to ask God for what you want because it will be for what he wants also

☑ What does God's promise of assurance (v. 33) mean to you?

29

DARE TO RISK

❏ If you have not already done so, what will it take to get you to let go of your possessions and get out of the boat with your material needs? Be specific.

use Peter as an example in your life:

When Peter got out of the boat to go to Jesus, he wasn't thinking about taking anything with him. He probably wanted to be as light as possible. To walk on water, Peter had to leave his possessions in the boat. To try to swim to Jesus with a backpack would have been silly enough. But to try to walk on water with baggage would have been even more ridiculous.

Yet, isn't that what we sometimes do when we try to follow Jesus? We pack stuff into our lives, make provision for ourselves, save up for a "rainy day." The problem is that all these things make it difficult to get out of the boat. We know that to carry our material possessions with us is almost certain death. To be willing to leave them behind means total dependence on God, and we're not always sure we're capable of that. To open ourselves up to material needs can open us up to all kinds of worry.

But refusing to trust God with our material needs prevents us from being obedient. And not trusting that God will provide when we experience material needs causes anxiety. Both demonstrate lack of faith and an ultimate trust in our own ability to provide for ourselves. The lesson from the sparrows, the lilies, and Peter is that the One who calls us out of the boat knows what we need to sustain ourselves; when we follow where He leads, He promises to provide for our material needs. *Read Hebrews 13:5-6*

the end

GROWING BY DOING

Things to think about for the week

In groups of three, grapple with the question, "What is one thing that I can do this week to demonstrate my willingness to trust God with my possessions and get out of the boat with my material needs?"

GETTING OUT OF THE BOAT WITH OUR MATERIAL NEEDS

GOING THE SECOND MILE

Before leaving this session, commit to doing one thing this week which will demonstrate your willingness to trust God more with your finances and material possessions. Work out a plan of action to make sure you follow through on your commitment. Be prepared to share what you did when you meet with the group next time.

Memorize Hebrews 13:5-6:

[5]Keep your lives free from the love of money and be content with what you have, because God has said, "Never will I leave you; never will I forsake you." [6]So we say with confidence, "The Lord is my helper; I will not be afraid. What can man do to me?"

EXECUTIVE
FISHERMAN
ASSOCIATION
FISHERS
OF
MEN
ASSOCIATION

FOUR

Getting Out of the Boat with Our Careers

GroupSpeak: *"Whenever I meet people for the first time, they almost always ask the question, 'What do you do?' It's no wonder so much of my identity is tied up with my job. I find myself wanting to give a response that impresses or at least is acceptable to them."*

"What Do You Do?"
When asked the question, "What do you do?" how do you reply? Teacher? Engineer? Salesperson? Homemaker? Mechanic? Bookkeeper? Retired? Rather than saying, "I teach," a person usually says, "I'm a teacher." Rather than responding with, "I repair cars," another says, "I'm a mechanic." There is little doubt that most of us define who we are by what we do for a living. We easily forget that as Christians our primary identity is in Christ. Our relationship with Him, not our careers or jobs, is what is supposed to shape how we see ourselves.

When asked questions about who we are, however, few of us respond immediately with our God-given identity in mind. Rarely, if ever, do we tell someone, "I'm a follower of Jesus and a child and servant in the kingdom of God." That we don't even think of this response tells us something significant about ourselves and our relationship with the Lord. And it holds implications for taking risks in faith and obedience when it comes to our careers.

How does God want us to look at our careers and jobs in light of our identity and relationship to Him? How do our attitudes toward what we do for a living affect our ability to get out of the boat and be totally available for the Lord's purposes? What can we learn from Peter and the other disciples who left their careers to follow Jesus? How can we become more open to risk-taking in this important area of our lives?

Work and Me
Reflect on the following questions, then share your responses with the group.

❑ How did you come to be in your career or current position?

❑ How much do you enjoy what you do for a living?

❑ How hard would it be for you to give up what you do, and why?

GAINING INSIGHT

From Fishermen to Followers
Read aloud Matthew 4:18-22.

¹⁸As Jesus was walking beside the Sea of Galilee, He saw two brothers, Simon called Peter and his brother Andrew. They were casting a net into the lake, for they were fishermen. ¹⁹"Come, follow Me," Jesus said, "and I will make

GETTING OUT OF THE BOAT WITH OUR CAREERS

you fishers of men." ²⁰At once they left their nets and followed Him.

²¹Going on from there, He saw two other brothers, James son of Zebedee and his brother John. They were in a boat with their father Zebedee, preparing their nets. Jesus called them, ²²and immediately they left the boat and their father and followed Him.

Matthew 4:18-22

❑ What type of career did Peter and his brother Andrew have?

❑ What did Jesus tell Peter and Andrew?

❑ What do you think Jesus meant by, "Follow Me, and I will make you fishers of men"?

❑ What did this career move mean for Peter, Andrew, James, and John?

❑ Knowing what you do from the New Testament, what was the outcome of the decision these fishermen made?

DARE TO RISK

☐ If you had been at the Sea of Galilee with these fishermen, what feelings, fears, or obstacles would have hindered you from following Jesus when He called your name?

☐ In what ways do you suppose Peter's clear decision to become a follower of Jesus at this point affected his ability later to get out of the boat and walk on water?

GROWING BY DOING

☐ What is the primary source of your identity? To what extent does it come from being a follower of Jesus and how much does it come from your career, job, or occupation?

☐ In what ways does your current career or job affect your obedience to God and taking risks in faith?

☐ With reference to your job or career, what attitude change or action is God asking you to make? How will you concretely respond to Him?

GOING THE SECOND MILE

Encouragement and motivation to take risks in faith often come when we learn about others who have acted in obedience in similar circumstances. This assignment is intended to

GETTING OUT OF THE BOAT WITH OUR CAREERS

help us meet others who have already gotten out of the boat with their careers and are "walking on water" by faith in this area of their lives.

During the week find at least one person who has made a significant career change based on God's calling or who clearly lives out his or her faith on the job in a secular environment. Ask questions like the following to help you gain information and insight.

- ❏ How did God guide you in your decision to change careers?
- ❏ What specific things enabled you to get out of the boat with your career and trust God with it?
- ❏ What counsel can you give me as I seek to be obedient and take risks in faith with my career or job?

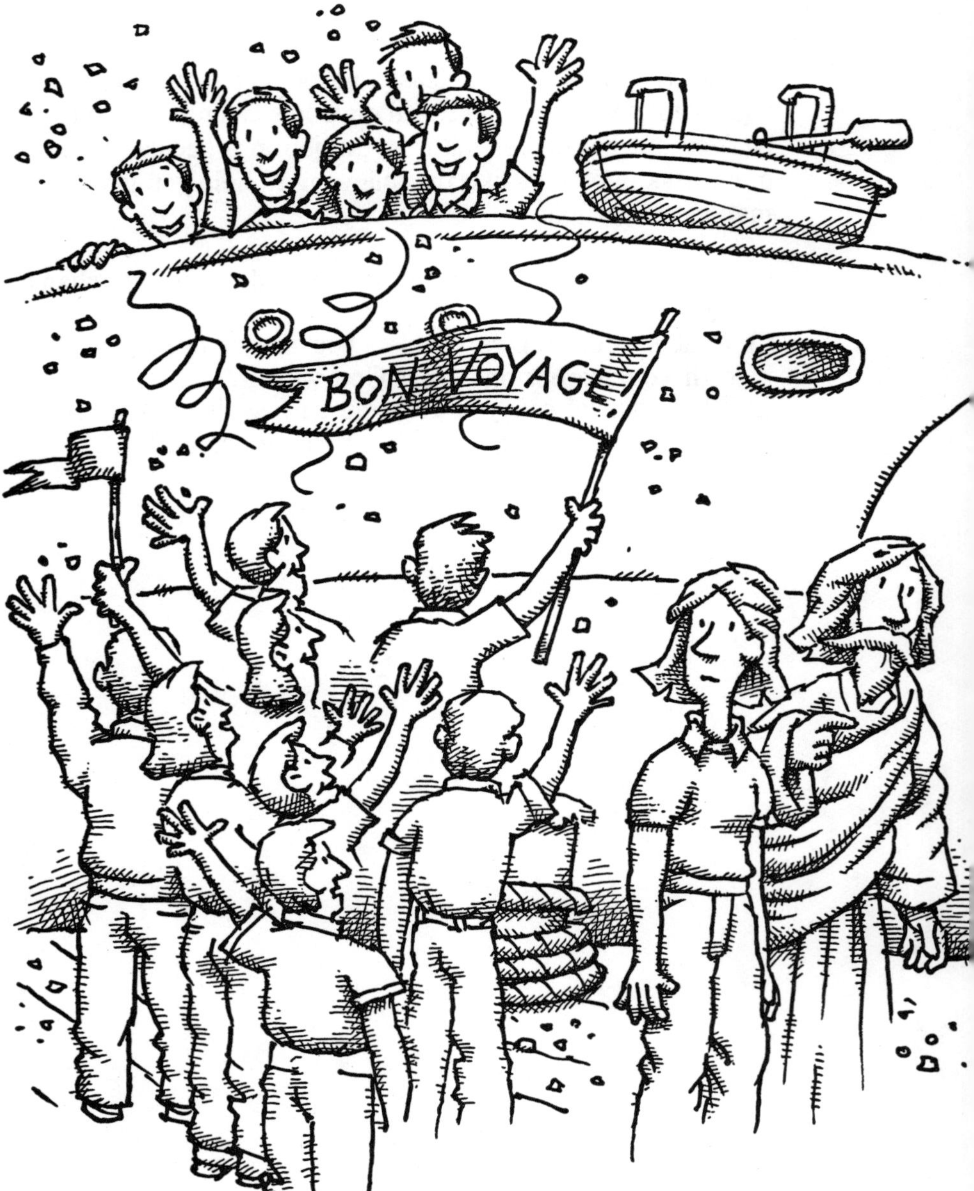
BON VOYAGE!

FIVE

Getting Out of the Boat with Our Relationships

GroupSpeak: *"My relationships influence me so much. Even though I'm an adult, the opinions of my family still affect me. My decisions and actions are influenced by what my friends think. Pressures to please others make it really hard to put God first."*

Significant Others

Ward, June, Wally, and Beaver Cleaver. Charlie Brown and Lucy. Laverne and Shirley. Ricky, Lucy, Fred, and Ethel. Romeo and Juliet. "The Golden Girls." Spouses, parents, children, siblings, coworkers, neighbors, lovers, and friends. These are just some of the relationships that make up our lives. They bring us our greatest joy and often our deepest pain. They not only influence what we do but who we are.

God created us to be social beings. We were meant to be in relationship with God and with one another. Much of our identity is shaped by our relationships. Some relationships, whether with family or friends, add tremendously to our character and Christian growth. Others take on such importance that they actually become idols to us; they take priority over our relationship with God. Following the Lord means making

DARE TO RISK

a choice to put Him first, even at the risk of losing the security and comfort we derive from the people we love. We need to learn how to let go and discover that in potentially losing these relationships we gain so much more.

GETTING ACQUAINTED

Ship and Shore
Just like us, the people in our lives are at their own points in their relationship with Jesus Christ. Some have committed their lives to Him and, by doing so, are "in the boat." Others are like Peter. We admire them because they seem to "walk on water" in faith and obedience to God. Still others remain on shore, yet to make a decision to ask Jesus into their lives and climb on board. Regardless of where these people are in their relationship with God, because they are important to us, they influence who we are and what we do. This exercise is intended to help us think through how these people help or hinder us from exercising more faith in our walk with God.

- ❏ List 10–15 persons who play a significant part in your life.
- ❏ Underline the names of all those who are "in the boat" (Christians).
- ❏ Place a star by the names of those Christians you consider to be "out of the boat," with lives characterized by "walking on water" in faith and obedience to God.
- ❏ Circle the names of those who are still on shore (not yet Christians).

Who's Number One?
Taking an honest assessment, on a scale of 0 to 10, with 10 being highest, rate your relationships according to how they tend to influence your decisions and actions. For each type of relationship listed, place a circle around the mark beneath the appropriate number. What does the assessment tell you about the priority you give certain relationships?

	0	1	2	3	4	5	6	7	8	9	10
Father:	—	—	—	—	—	—	—	—	—	—	—
Mother:	—	—	—	—	—	—	—	—	—	—	—
Spouse:	—	—	—	—	—	—	—	—	—	—	—

GETTING OUT OF THE BOAT WITH OUR RELATIONSHIPS

	0	1	2	3	4	5	6	7	8	9	10
Brother(s):	—	—	—	—	—	—	—	—	—	—	—
Sister(s):	—	—	—	—	—	—	—	—	—	—	—
Children:	—	—	—	—	—	—	—	—	—	—	—
Grandmother:	—	—	—	—	—	—	—	—	—	—	—
Grandfather:	—	—	—	—	—	—	—	—	—	—	—
Other relative:	—	—	—	—	—	—	—	—	—	—	—
Pastor:	—	—	—	—	—	—	—	—	—	—	—
Best friend(s):	—	—	—	—	—	—	—	—	—	—	—
God:	—	—	—	—	—	—	—	—	—	—	—
Other:	—	—	—	—	—	—	—	—	—	—	—

GAINING INSIGHT

Cost of Discipleship

Matthew 10:37-39 focuses on the priority of our relationship with God over the other relationships in our lives. He demands and deserves our undivided loyalty, and Jesus, here in this passage, in no uncertain terms, tells His twelve disciples that the cost of following Him is complete, wholehearted allegiance to Him. When He calls us to follow Him, He demands no less.

One of our difficulties in following Jesus is often our relationships. They tend to prevent us from taking risks in faith because we place higher priority on them than being obedient to God. The text for this session not only challenges us to get out of the boat with our relationships but gives us assurance that, when we do, we gain far more than we ever lose.

Read Matthew 10:37-39.

[37]**Anyone who loves his father or mother more than Me is not worthy of Me; anyone who loves his son or daughter more than Me is not worthy of Me;** [38]**and anyone who does not take his cross and follow Me is not worthy of Me.** [39]**Whoever finds his life will lose it, and whoever loses his life for My sake will find it.**

Matthew 10:37-39

DARE TO RISK

❑ What do you think Jesus meant when He said that those loving father, mother, son, or daughter more than Him are not worthy of Him?

One Greek-English lexicon translates the phrase, "not worthy of Me" as "does not deserve to belong to Me." How does this help clarify the meaning of Jesus' statement?

Initially, when we are born, we see ourselves as belonging to our parents. We grow up under their care, and our sense of identity is shaped by their influence. When we become Christians, God tells us that we must put Him first. We now belong to Him; we are adopted children of His, and He is now our Parent whom we are to obey. Our love for Him is to take precedence over our love for our families. Whether we are only children of parents or also parents with children, the fact remains that Jesus is to be more important to us than they are.

God is not asking us to disown our families. He is not saying, don't care about them. Rather, He is warning us about the cost of our commitment to Him. When a choice has to be made between obeying Him or following their wishes or needs, He expects us to choose Him.

❑ Look again at how you rated your relationships in importance and priority. What is affirming or convicting about your ratings? What place does God have in your life right now? How do you feel about it?

The command, "Take up the cross and follow Me" is a familiar one to most of us. The cross was associated with death and suffering. Indeed, just prior to Jesus' words here, He speaks of coming persecutions (Matthew 10:16-32) and what life as His disciple is like.

❑ What do you think it means to take up the cross and follow Jesus today?

In verse 39, Jesus speaks of "finding" one's life. The Greek word for "find" seems to indicate the idea of obtaining rather than uncovering or encountering. It may be related to the idea of keeping for oneself. The phrase, "for My sake" in this same verse means "because of, on account of, for the sake of."

❑ How are we to understand the paradox that one who finds his life will lose it, and one who loses his life for Jesus' sake will find it? (v. 39)

Missionary Jim Elliot was martyred by the Auca Indians in Ecuador. He risked his life for the Gospel because he understood the meaning of Jesus' words: "Whoever finds his life will lose it, and whoever loses his life for My sake will find it." In his diary he wrote, "He is no fool who gives what he knows he cannot keep, to gain what he knows he cannot lose."

❑ How have you found this paradox to be true in your own life?

Taking up your cross means voluntarily choosing to walk the way of death. Jesus said, "Follow Me." Where did He go? To Calvary, but the story doesn't stop there. God went on to raise Him from the dead, and He is now seated with His Father in the heavens. When we take up the cross, it is not an end in itself either. We are also promised resurrection from the dead and life everlasting. Death must come before resurrection. Losing our life for Christ's sake must come before we find our true life. We must die to self in order to become alive in Christ. We must be ready to let go of existing human relationships when Jesus calls us onto the water. Only as we risk losing the security we derive from them, do we find real security in God. If Peter hadn't been willing to leave his friends in the boat, he never would have walked on water.

Relationships may be the hardest thing to let go of because they define who we are. To "find your own life" is to define your identity by your relationships. And that is what we naturally do. We are born into a family that gives us our primary identity and allegiance. A big part of the cost of following Jesus is switching primary allegiance. The cross represents that switching of allegiance and total commitment to Him. It represents dying to all the other things we use to define who we are. Belonging to Christ means we are no longer our own. But that's not bad news. It's good news! If we put our relationship with God first and gain our identity from Him instead of others, we discover who we really are and are meant to be.

GROWING BY DOING

Share your responses to the following two questions:

❏ What relationships do you feel you would jeopardize or risk losing if you became more obedient or faithful to God?

❏ How do you intend to think or act differently in those relationships in light of what God has revealed to you this session?

GETTING OUT OF THE BOAT WITH OUR RELATIONSHIPS

After completing your discussion, pray for each other.

GOING THE SECOND MILE

From your own knowledge of Scripture, select a Bible character who risked his or her relationships in order to obey God. Prepare a three- to five-minute lesson to share with the group at the next meeting. Include the circumstances of the person, the risk, the outcome, and the reason you selected him or her.

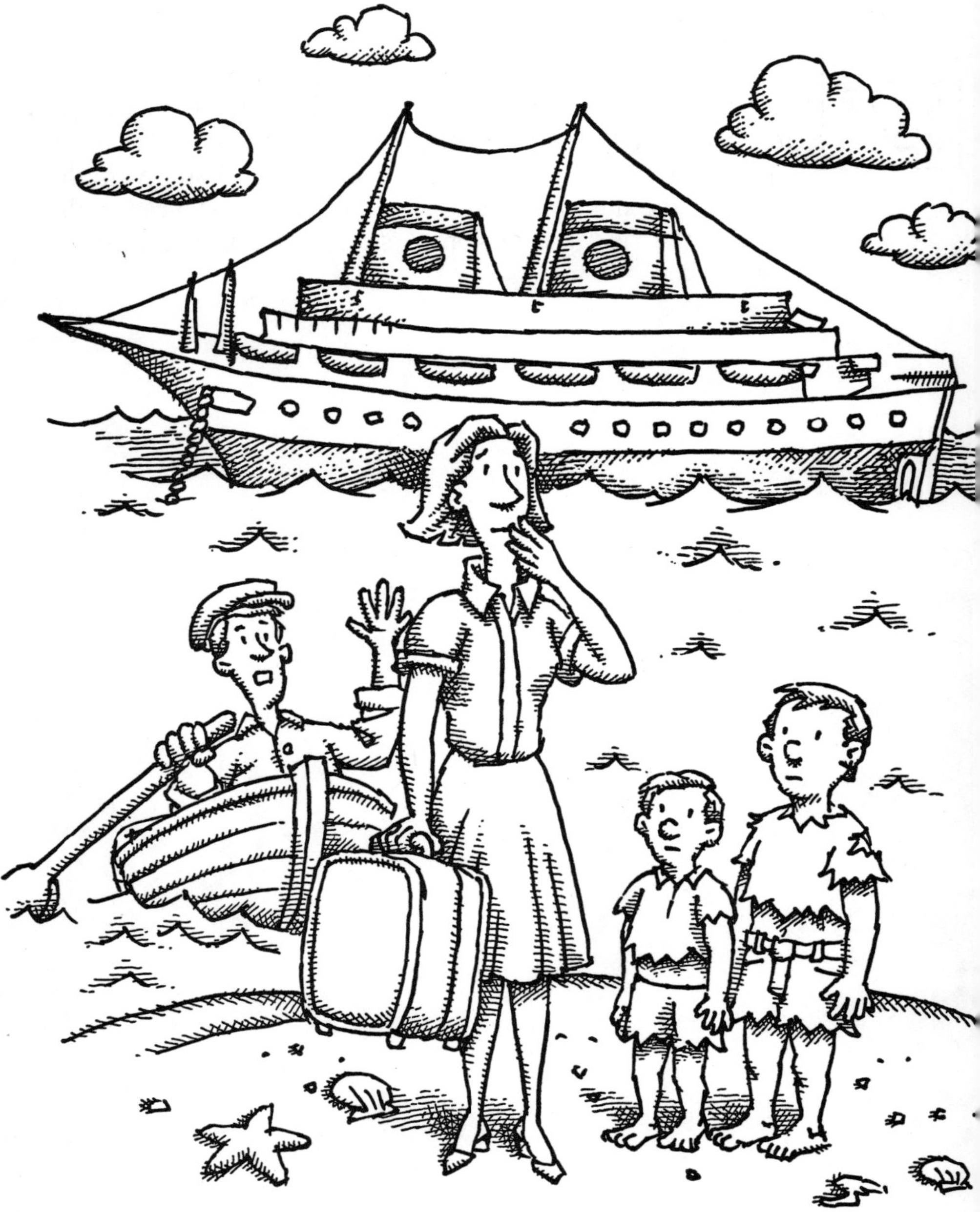

SIX

Getting Out of the Boat with Our Convictions

GroupSpeak: *"I know about the passages in the Bible that talk about helping the poor, feeding the hungry, working for social justice, and fighting oppression. And I believe that doing these things, not just believing in them, is part of what it means to be a Christian. But I find myself wanting to shy away from getting involved."*

On Uneasy Street

Near Los Angeles, in April 1992, a jury acquitted four white police officers of charges that they had used excessive and unnecessary force to arrest an African-American man. Someone with a video camera had captured the incident on tape, and the clip of the beating shown on the news seemed to indicate an unfair verdict. Enraged by the apparent injustice, thousands of people reacted with rioting, arson, killing, and looting. In a matter of a couple of days, parts of Los Angeles were in ruins.

What were we to make of this? What was to be a Christian response to the violence? What could believers do to make the presence of Christ felt in such a situation? How could they be salt and light not only during the crisis but in the affected communities long-term?

DARE TO RISK

These are the kinds of questions we should always be asking whenever and wherever we see people in need of the love of Christ. Jesus' own ministry reflected a central concern for the poor, the needy, and the oppressed. He ministered in both word and deed to them.

For many of us, however, following in Jesus' footsteps can be a bit frightening. His ministry was primarily in the streets, not the synagogues. If we follow Him, He may lead us into the ghettos, prisons, and back alleys of our cities. We may find ourselves meeting strangers who are homeless, teenagers who are prostitutes, babies who are malnourished, addicts who are looking for their next fix. These people live way outside our comfort zones.

Yet they are the people for whom Christ came and died. And He has commanded us to continue to carry out His ministry with them, a ministry which takes all kinds of risks in faith and obedience. If we haven't already, how many of us are ready to get out of the boat in this area of discipleship?

GETTING ACQUAINTED

First Things First?

Someone once said that trying to meet the needs of the poor in this world is like trying to rearrange deck chairs on the *Titanic*. Since people are going to hell every day, the most important thing to do is to try to save as many souls as possible.

❑ To what extent do you agree or disagree with this opinion, and why?

Personal Assessment

❑ What are you now doing to live out your convictions regarding ministry to your community and world?

❑ How satisfied are you with your ministry in this area?

GETTING OUT OF THE BOAT WITH OUR CONVICTIONS

❏ If you are not satisfied, what must happen to change your level of satisfaction?

❏ What would it take for you to become more involved in ministry to your community and the world?

GAINING INSIGHT
Doers of the Word
Convictions come in all shapes and forms. They are strong beliefs we hold about such things as our relationship with God, our families, our careers, politics, and human nature and rights. God has given us Scripture to inform about the convictions and values He wants us to possess. As Christians, it is our responsibility to not only embrace them but to seek to live them out.

However, such responsibility is not easy. Some convictions are more difficult to hold and live out than others, like those related to justice, equality, compassion, sharing, and peacemaking. We find it hard to translate our convictions in these areas into actions like feeding the hungry, being an advocate for the oppressed and powerless, seeking to eliminate racism and sexism. We're often left feeling guilty, callous, or discouraged.

Silently read James 2:14-17. As you do, what feelings do you experience?

¹⁴"What good is it, my brothers, if a man claims to have faith but has no deeds? Can such faith save him? ¹⁵Suppose a brother or sister is without clothes and daily food. ¹⁶If one of you says to him, "Go, I wish you well; keep warm and well fed," but does nothing about his physical needs, what good is it? ¹⁷In the same way, faith by itself, if it is not accompanied by action, is dead.

James 2:14-17

DARE TO RISK

The Miracle of Multiplication

Jesus' compassion often moved Him to acts of mercy and kindness. When He saw a need, He felt compassion, and the compassion moved Him to action. Sometimes He healed the sick or cast out demons (Matthew 14:14). Other times His compassion resulted in teaching the lost about the kingdom of God (Mark 6:34). Read about His compassion for a hungry crowd of 4,000 in Mark 8:1-10.

¹During those days another large crowd gathered. Since they had nothing to eat, Jesus called His disciples to Him and said, ²"I have compassion for these people; they have already been with me three days and have nothing to eat. ³If I send them home hungry, they will collapse on the way, because some of them have come a long distance."

⁴His disciples answered, "But where in this remote place can anyone get enough bread to feed them?"

⁵"How many loaves do you have?" Jesus asked. "Seven," they replied.

⁶He told the crowd to sit down on the ground. When He had taken the seven loaves and given thanks, He broke them and gave them to His disciples to set before the people, and they did so. ⁷They had a few small fish as well; He gave thanks for them also and told the disciples to distribute them. ⁸The people ate and were satisfied. Afterward the disciples picked up seven basketfuls of broken pieces that were left over. ⁹About four thousand men were present. And having sent them away, ¹⁰He got into the boat with His disciples and went to the region of Dalmanutha.

Mark 8:1-10

❏ What does Jesus' compassion allow Him to see?

Note that Jesus' compassion not only enables Him to see others' needs but to acknowledge His responsibility to meet those needs. He could have simply taught the people for three days and then sent them away. Yet, He was concerned about their total well-being. He told His disciples, "If I send them home hungry, they will collapse on the way, because some of them have come a long distance" (v. 3).

Jesus did not simply present the Gospel message and ignore the physical needs of those to whom He preached. He ministered to the whole person. He felt a responsibility to feed both their bodies and spirits. His actions toward them grew out of the compassion He felt for them. For Jesus, compassion was love in action. The Gospel message was both proclamation and demonstration of the love of God.

❏ What objection do the disciples raise to feeding the people?

When Jesus speaks of feeding the crowds, the disciples naturally raise objections. They question how it can be done. The circumstances indicate that it's not possible. After all, they're in a remote place and just don't have the resources.

Once we identify a need, one of the major obstacles to meeting it is our lack of trust in God's provision. We become overwhelmed by the circumstances and the enormity of the need. We fail to walk by faith and instead walk by sight. When we look at the need with the eyes of "what is" we conclude, "We don't have enough money or time." It's only when we look at the need with the eyes of faith that we see what God can provide to meet the need.

❏ What excuses do you tend to use when trying to avoid meeting a need you see in the world? List some of the "I don't have enough . . ." statements you use.

DARE TO RISK

❑ What did Jesus do when the disciples offered Him the food they had?

In this story we discover that when we offer to God whatever we have, however little it may seem, He blesses and multiplies it. When the disciples gave Jesus the bread and fish, He took and blessed the food and gave it back to the disciples for distribution. As stewards of what they had been given, the disciples offered the bread and fish to others.

The disciples gave Jesus the little food they had. We may need to offer Jesus our time, our education, our money, our possessions, our freedom, or our power to influence. Whatever it is, He wants to receive, transform, and use it to minister to those in the world around us.

❑ What were the explicit and implicit outcomes of the feeding of the 4,000?

The story tells us that not only was everyone fed, but an abundance of food remained. This fact speaks to those of us who fear that if we give up what we have to God on behalf of others, we won't have enough for ourselves. On the contrary, God takes what we give to Him and multiplies it in a way that leads to overflowing in blessings, resources, and praise.

❑ What are some lessons you can glean from this story?

❑ How does this story encourage you to "get out of the boat" to do more acts of mercy, justice, and compassion?

GETTING OUT OF THE BOAT WITH OUR CONVICTIONS

❏ What is God asking *you* to give Him to help meet a need in your community or the world? What "loaves" is Jesus asking you to offer Him? How will you respond?

GROWING BY DOING

Ready, Set, Go!
Brainstorm all the different ways we could live out our convictions to seek the welfare of the poor and needy. Think of things that can be done both individually and as a group, one time and on-going. Be concrete and specific, naming places, agencies, and organizations. Then select one activity to do as a group project. It doesn't have to be conducted before the next meeting, but it should be completed before the end of session 8.

Pray for the project and the specific needs of the community and world identified in the brainstorming.

GOING THE SECOND MILE

During the week, pray about the "loaves" you think God is asking you to offer Him to meet a need in your community. Think about how these "loaves" can be used specifically in your small group project.

Find out about one social service agency or an ongoing church-sponsored community project that interests you. Obtain and write down pertinent information about it, including the name of the project, purpose, target group, address, telephone number, contact person, and any other helpful material you uncover. Turn in your information sheet at the next meeting so that a directory or resource guide to social concerns activities can be compiled for your group or church.

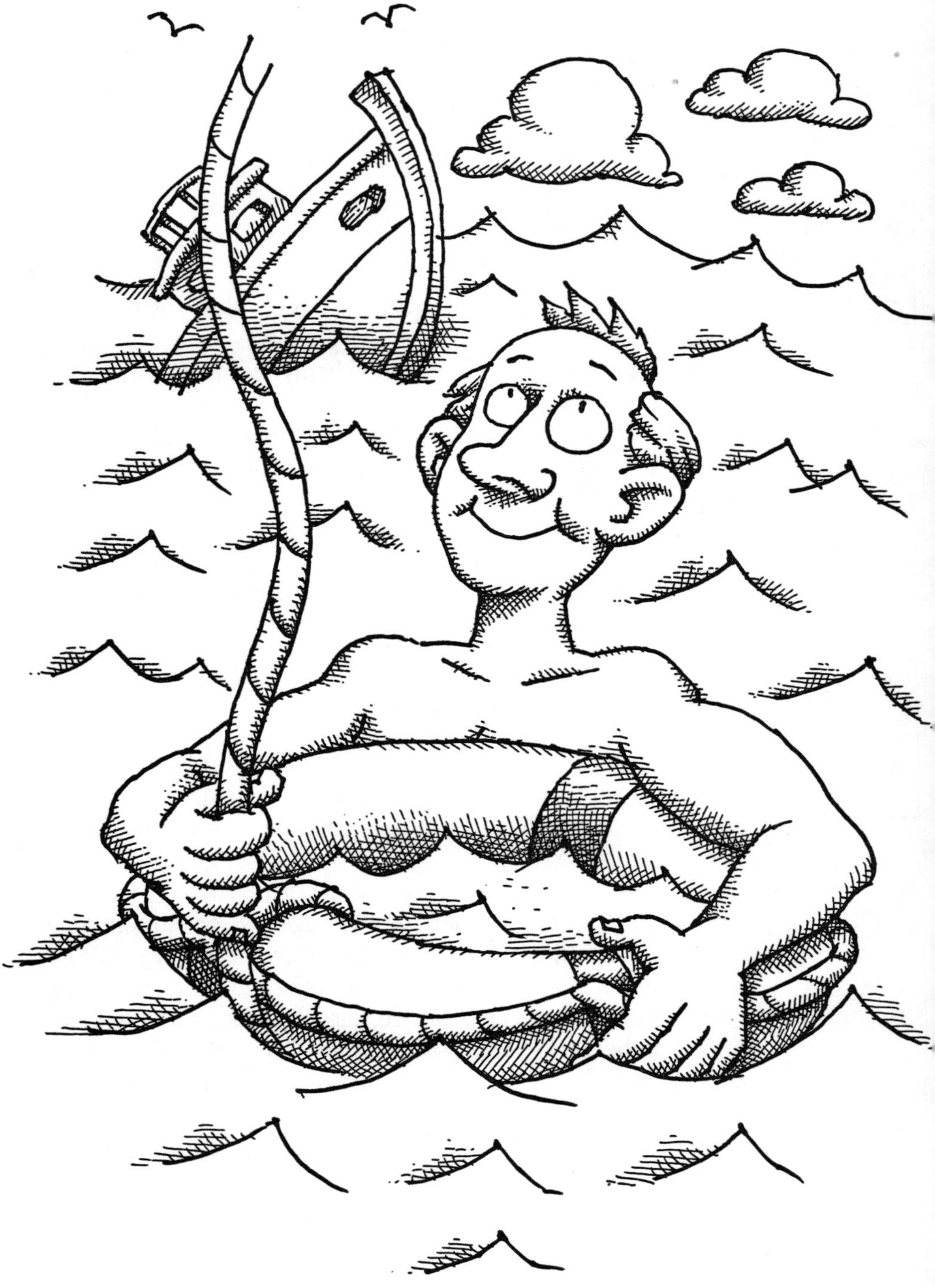

SEVEN

Staying Afloat with God

GroupSpeak: *"Even if I trust God and get out of the boat and take a risk in faith to be obedient to Him, I have this fear that once I do it, I won't be able to keep going. I'll drown. I know that unless I have a growing relationship with God, I won't be able to stay afloat when things get rough. How can I keep quality fellowship with Him?"*

The Other Half of the Story

Getting out of the boat in a specific area of our lives is a faith-building experience. As God takes us out of our comfort zones, we discover the thrill of finding our life even as we lose it; we know first-hand what Peter must have felt as he walked on the Sea of Galilee; we discover the joy of obedience, even in the midst of taking risks.

But all this is only half the story. The other half has to do with staying afloat once we're on the water. Invariably, the wind and waves come, just as they did for Peter. Doubt, discouragement, fear, and other obstacles distract us from trusting God. We get scared and want to return to the safety of the boat. What then? How do we keep our eyes fixed on Jesus and continue to move ahead?

DARE TO RISK

GETTING ACQUAINTED

Up Close and Personal
Name one person with whom you have a very close relationship.

List some of the characteristics of your relationship, including how you became so intimate.

How does your relationship with the other person get you through the difficult times in life?

How is your relationship with God similar or different from your relationship with this person?

What things do you do personally to develop a closer relationship with God?

GAINING INSIGHT

Experiencing Solitude
Quiet times, daily devotions, Bible study, prayer, small groups, retreats, worship. These are some of the things that we as Christians engage in as a way to develop our relationship with God. Another one is the discipline of solitude. It is less familiar to many of us but no less important.

Take the next 10 minutes to find a quiet place alone. Do not read, talk to others, or do anything but sit in God's presence. Focus on experiencing fellowship with Him. Be still until the leader calls you back to the group.

After regathering, share your responses to these questions:

❏ What feelings did you experience during your time alone with God?

❏ Other than your daily devotional times, what intentional or extended periods of time have you experienced being alone with God? How have they affected your relationship with God?

None of us would doubt the importance of daily time with God. But given the pattern of Jesus in the Gospels, where it is recorded that He spent extended periods of time alone with God and in prayer, it seems that God desires more than our relatively short daily devotions. He wants us to develop the kind of relationship that comes from extended periods of time alone with Him.

Think about being married. Think about the relationship between husband and wife. They see each other every day and talk about "maintenance" of the household and problems and decisions that require immediate attention. For many of us, this kind of interaction somewhat parallels our quiet times with God.

In marriage, it is also helpful to have another kind of interaction. It happens when it's just the husband and wife, away from the house for an evening or perhaps a weekend. These are the times when they can be face-to-face, enjoy one another's company, do some evaluation, and gain perspective and refreshment. In solitude, there is a similar kind of interaction with God.

DARE TO RISK

For most of us, daily quiet times are not enough. Squeezed into a busy day, they are inadequate to keep our relationship with the Lord healthy or our eyes fixed on Him. This is why the discipline of solitude is so important.

Solitude is not simply being alone. It is being alone with God. One author describes solitude as a "precious, fearless space where we are aware that we belong to God" (Donald Postema, *Space for God,* Bible Way, 1983). Solitude is retreating from the world and entreating the Lord to make Himself known. It is withdrawing from the distractions of the world and drawing near to the heart of God. It is looking beyond the wind and the waves in our lives to see clearly the face of Jesus before us.

Retreating to Move Ahead
In more than one place in the Gospel accounts, the writers record that Jesus engaged in solitude. Recall that the night before Peter walked on water, Jesus, "after He had dismissed the crowds, went up the mountain by Himself to pray" (Matthew 14:23, NRSV).

Jesus told His disciples that He did nothing except that which His Father told Him to do (John 5:19; 14:10). And in order to know what that was, He spoke with the Father and listened to Him through prayer. Jesus was able to keep obedient to the will and work of His Father in heaven by spending quality time alone with Him. In Mark 1:35-39 we are given a picture of what Jesus' practice of solitude was like and the outcome it had on His life and ministry.

[35]Very early in the morning, while it was still dark, Jesus got up, left the house and went off to a solitary place, where He prayed. [36]Simon and his companions went to look for Him, [37]and when they found Him, they exclaimed: "Everyone is looking for You!"

[38]Jesus replied, "Let us go somewhere else—to the nearby villages—so I can preach there also. That is why I have come." [39]So He traveled throughout Galilee, preaching in their synagogues and driving out demons.
                                                  Mark 1:35-39

❑ What do you observe about Jesus' practice of the discipline of solitude? (v. 35)

❑ What kinds of principles might you draw about the discipline of solitude, given verse 35?

❑ What did Jesus tell His companions after they found Him? Then what did He do?

❑ Given what is recorded in verses 38 and 39, what do you think was the outcome of Jesus' time of solitude with God?

The fruits of solitude are many. One is that we gain perspective and discern God's will. Taking time out from busyness allows us to see where we've been, where we are, and where we're going in life. In the quietness that solitude creates, it is easier to hear the still, small voice of God as He seeks to direct, correct, or confirm our course. This is one of the reasons Jesus often arose early and went away to that solitary place to pray. He needed to ask for His Father's guidance and power for the work He had been given to do. Recall how before Jesus chose His twelve disciples, He spent an entire night alone with God in prayer (Luke 6:12-16). As we find ourselves out on the water, we need to be as diligent in speaking with and listening to our Heavenly Father.

Solitude also offers a wonderful source of refreshment. The Apostle Paul speaks of the Christian life as a race and how we need to endure and persevere; we're to run in such a way that we finish. The discipline of solitude provides extended rest stops for us along our spiritual journey, where we can unhurriedly drink of the Living Water (John 7:37-39), and gain refreshment for our souls. Risk-taking can be energy draining, and solitude can help to replenish our reserves.

A third fruit of solitude is empowerment for ministry and the things God has called us to do. By spending time with Him in solitude, we develop a greater confidence in who He is and what He desires to do through us. We get to know Him and ourselves better. Doing so makes it easier to take risks because we are doing it for someone we really know and trust. As our relationship with God is built through solitude, our obedience finds its source more and more in love for Him rather than in mere duty.

In addition, in solitude we are able to let go of the things that weigh us down. We let go and become filled with the Spirit of God. Rid of the excess weight, we are able to walk on water with greater ease.

❑ What are some of your personal thoughts and feelings about practicing the discipline of solitude in your own life?

GROWING BY DOING

Using the suggestions given to you by the leader, spend the next few minutes thinking through how you can begin to practice the discipline of solitude in your own life on a regular basis. Write down the possibilities and commit to one thing you will do during the week.

When the leader indicates, share your plan of action with one other person, and then pray for each other.

GOING THE SECOND MILE

In preparation for next time, come prepared to share what you did in this area of solitude. Also, write down your responses to these two questions:

❑ Right now, what is one area where you feel you are walking on water?

❑ How do you see the discipline of solitude helping you to stay afloat as you take risks in faith and obedience to God in this area?

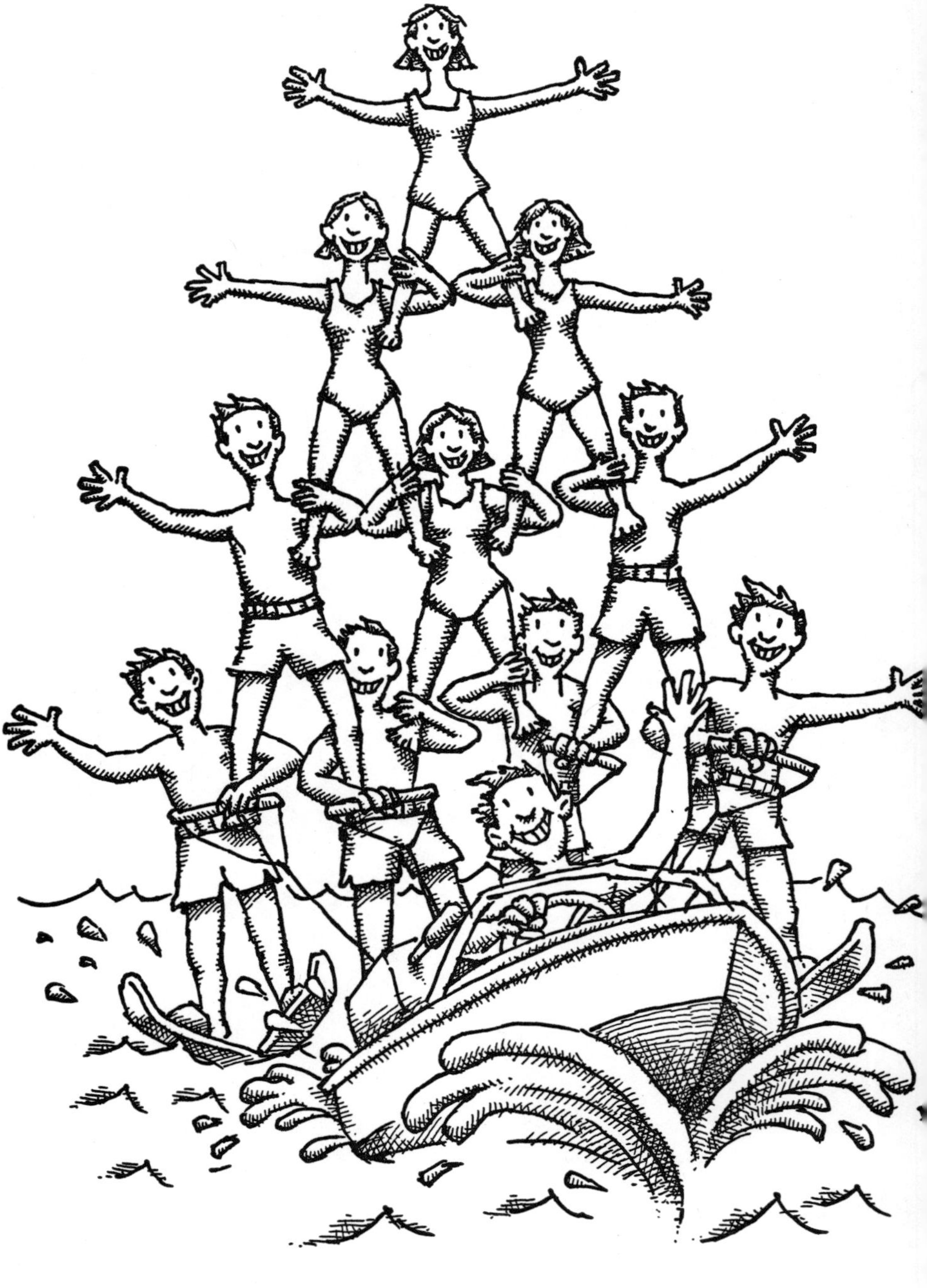

EIGHT

*Staying Afloat
with the Community of Faith*

GroupSpeak: *"I can see the value of being in relationship with other Christians who are serious about living out their faith. It's hard to develop new attitudes and behaviors by yourself. I need the accountability that can come with brothers and sisters in Christ. But sometimes these people are hard to find."*

Cocooning or Community?
Ever heard of "cocooning"? It's a relatively new term used to describe the way Americans live these days. People tend to spend less and less time outside their homes. With things like home delivery of food, mail order catalogs, videotape rentals, and modems, people have less need to venture outside. And many are kept inside because of fear of being mugged on the street or robbed while away.

Cocooning makes it difficult to establish meaningful relationships with others. It leads to isolation, alienation, and loneliness. Cocooning hinders the development of a sense of community even among Christians. We know we need fellowship, but unless we are intentional about seeking it, we often find ourselves without ongoing support and accountability from our brothers and sisters in Christ.

As we think about risk-taking in the Christian life, we need to ask ourselves a number of questions: Can we be risk-takers apart from belonging to a caring community of faith? Who will God use to rescue us when we get distracted and begin drowning as we walk on water? Who will He use when we become weary, panicky, and take our eyes off Jesus? Just as we need time alone in fellowship with God to keep us going and growing, we need fellowship with others in the community of faith to help us remain faithful and obedient to God.

GETTING ACQUAINTED

Solo and Several

Last session we looked at solitude. The flip side of solitude is community. So much of Scripture uses relational language. God Himself is engaged in community. Consider the Godhead. There is a "we-ness," an interdependence about the relationships among the Father, Son, and Holy Spirit. At Creation God said, "Let Us make man in Our image, in Our likeness (Genesis 1:26). Implicit in this interdependence that is demonstrated at Creation is a unity among the Three in One, a communion or community. They model it for us.

As people created in God's image, we are social and relational creatures. Since His nature is relational in essence, those whom He created are also relational by design. Humans were meant to relate to God and to their fellow beings. We were meant to experience both solitude and community.

As you think about the corporate aspect of the Christian life, how would you answer these questions?

❑ What does the phrase "Christian community" mean to you?

❑ When have you experienced Christian community, and what was it like?

STAYING AFLOAT WITH THE COMMUNITY OF FAITH

GAINING INSIGHT

Characteristics of Community
Read Colossians 3:12-17.

> ¹²Therefore, as God's chosen people, holy and dearly loved, clothe yourselves with compassion, kindness, humility, gentleness and patience. ¹³Bear with each other and forgive whatever grievances you may have against one another. Forgive as the Lord forgave you. ¹⁴And over all these virtues put on love, which binds them all together in perfect unity.
>
> ¹⁵Let the peace of Christ rule in your hearts, since as members of one body you were called to peace. And be thankful. ¹⁶Let the Word of Christ dwell in you richly as you teach and admonish one another with all wisdom, and as you sing psalms, hymns and spiritual songs with gratitude in your hearts to God. ¹⁷And whatever you do, whether in word or deed, do it all in the name of the Lord Jesus, giving thanks to God the Father through Him.
>
> **Colossians 3:12-17**

❑ Who makes up the Christian community, and what does it mean to be holy and dearly loved?

❑ What qualities are God's "chosen people" to demonstrate, and why do you think these are so important in Christian community? (v. 12)

❑ What do you think it means to "bear with each other," and how does it relate to forgiving others?

❑ Are there people in your community of faith you have not forgiven? How is this affecting your experience of Christian community?

DARE TO RISK

❑ When Christians "clothe themselves" with love, what do they look like?

❑ How are you practicing the things mentioned in verses 15-17? What is one area in which you have seen growth in yourself recently?

Koinonia
Koinonia is the Greek word which is often translated into the English words *fellowship, communion, close relationship, participation,* and *sharing in something.* For example, we find it in 1 John 1:3: "We proclaim to you what we have seen and heard, so that you also may have fellowship (koinonia) with us. And our fellowship (koinonia) is with the Father and with His Son, Jesus Christ." Here, koinonia describes a special relationship in the Holy Spirit between God and humankind and in their relationships with one another.

To be "in Christ" means to be in community. With the New Covenant through Jesus Christ, God established a new creation, a new people to be His own. When Jesus calls individuals, He calls them to join this new community, referred to as the church. He called the Twelve to share their lives, not just with Him, but with each other. How they related to one another seems almost as important as how they related to Him. From their relationships, they learned interdependence, grew to share one another's burdens, and gained insights from each other's strengths.

❑ How did you experience interdependence, sharing burdens, and gaining of insights in this small group?

Jesus wanted His disciples to see themselves within the context of a community, always part of something beyond themselves. Even the way He taught them to pray, beginning with "Our Father," emphasized the importance of corporate identity. And look at the word "disciple" itself. Of all the references to it in the New Testament, it hardly ever appears in the singular. Our Lord never intended any Lone Ranger Christians.

Community is also necessary for us to be what God desires. As disciples of Jesus, we are to become like Him. Since no one person possesses all the qualities of Christ, it is important that we have a variety of people to disciple us and to help us grow and know Him better. We each reflect only a part of Jesus. But in Christian community, we are exposed to those who together give us a more complete picture of Christlikeness. Corporately we reflect the fullness of God.

❏ How did you gain a better picture of Christ as a result of your relationships with your fellow group members?

❏ How are you more like Christ as a result of your relationships in the small group? How has God changed you as a result of your participation in this small group?

Two Are Better Than One
Just as community is necessary for us to become the men and women of God that He desires, it is also necessary for us to do what He desires. Those in the community of faith help shape our obedience, hold us accountable, and pick us up when we fall. We are sustained by their prayers and their presence. They are often Christ to us. Ecclesiastes 4:9-10 reads:

9Two are better than one, because they have a good return for their work: 10If one falls down, his friend can help him up. But pity the man who falls and has no one to help him up!

❏ How has your own experience in this small group demonstrated the necessity and importance of the community of faith in your risk-taking and obedience to God?

DARE TO RISK

❑ In what ways, big or small, has God used this group to enable you to "walk on water" in a specific area of your life?

GROWING BY DOING
Passing the Blessing
Authors Gary Smalley and John Trent, in their book, *The Blessing,* identify five basic elements of a blessing. They write, "A family blessing begins with meaningful touching. It continues with a spoken message that pictures a special future for the individual being blessed, and one that is based on an active commitment to see the blessing come to pass" (p. 27).

Both Old and New Testaments are full of blessings. Isaac gave one to his son Jacob (Genesis 27). David blessed the people (2 Samuel 18). Jonathan bestowed blessings on David (1 Samuel 20). Jesus blessed little children (Mark 10:13-16). And the Apostle Paul wrote letters full of blessings, using words such as "May the grace of our Lord Jesus Christ be with your spirit" (Galatians 6:18, NRSV), and "May the God of peace Himself sanctify you entirely; and may your spirit and soul and body be kept sound and blameless at the coming of our Lord Jesus Christ" (1 Thessalonians 5:23, NRSV).

Take a few moments to think about the person whose name you have drawn. Then together, enjoy the blessings which will overflow in the group.

GOING THE SECOND MILE
What's Next?
Hebrews 10:24-25 reads:

[24]And let us consider how we may spur one another on toward love and good deeds. [25]Let us not give up meeting together, as some are in the habit of doing, but let us encourage one another — and all the more as you see the Day approaching.

If this small group has been a positive experience for you, there's no reason to let it end. Set up a time to meet with one or two other persons after this last session. The purpose may be simply for fellowship, or it may be to plan how to keep alive the community you have formed through this small group. The future is wide open. So take what you have learned through these eight sessions and walk on water together in obedience to God. Dare to risk! And discover again and again: The One who calls you out of the boat has the power to keep you afloat.

DEAR SMALL GROUP LEADER:

Picture Yourself As A Leader.

List some words that describe what would excite you or scare you as a leader of your small group.

A Leader Is Not...
❏ a person with all the answers.
❏ responsible for everyone having a good time.
❏ someone who does all the talking.
❏ likely to do everything perfectly.

A Leader Is...
❏ someone who encourages and enables group members to discover insights and build relationships.
❏ a person who helps others meet their goals, enabling the group to fulfill its purpose.
❏ a protector to keep members from being attacked or taken advantage of.
❏ the person who structures group time and plans ahead.
❏ the facilitator who stimulates relationships and participation by asking questions.
❏ an affirmer, encourager, challenger.

- [ ] enthusiastic about the small group, about God's Word, and about discovering and growing.

What Is Important To Small Group Members?
- [ ] A leader who cares about them.
- [ ] Building relationships with other members.
- [ ] Seeing themselves grow.
- [ ] Belonging and having a place in the group.
- [ ] Feeling safe while being challenged.
- [ ] Having their reasons for joining a group fulfilled.

What Do You Do . . .

If nobody talks—
- [ ] Wait—show the group members you expect them to answer.
- [ ] Rephrase a question—give them time to think.
- [ ] Divide into subgroups so all participate.

If somebody talks too much—
- [ ] Avoid eye contact with him or her.
- [ ] Sit beside the person next time. It will be harder for him or her to talk sitting by the leader.
- [ ] Suggest, "Let's hear from someone else."
- [ ] Interrupt with, "Great! Anybody else?"

If people don't know the Bible—
- [ ] Print out the passage in the same translation and hand it out to save time searching for a passage.
- [ ] Use the same Bible versions and give page numbers.
- [ ] Ask enablers to sit next to those who may need encouragement in sharing.
- [ ] Begin using this book to teach them how to study; affirm their efforts.

If you have a difficult individual—
- [ ] Take control to protect the group, but recognize that exploring differences can be a learning experience.
- [ ] Sit next to that person.
- [ ] To avoid getting sidetracked or to protect another group member, you may need to interrupt, saying, "Not all of us feel that way."
- [ ] Pray for that person before the group meeting.

ONE

The Challenge of Risk-Taking

Dare to Risk is intended to help believers to encourage one another to live out their faith in obedience to God even when that requires taking risks. Peter's experience when he got out of the boat to walk on the water to Jesus provides the framework for examining risk-taking in the Christian life. As you look at various aspects of your lives in the context of your small group, you will challenge each other to live out more fully your lives as disciples of Jesus Christ.

Risk-taking is moving out of our comfort zones. It often appears hazardous to our health. When God asks us to do something that seems too difficult for us, our response may be to resist or refuse to obey. The familiar is much easier.

As the group leader who facilitates discussions, responds to questions, and decides on which activities to guide the group through, you may feel like you're taking risks yourself. In this first session, you will be helping the group to get acquainted and discover their own risk-taking behavior. You have a choice as to which elements will best fit your group, your leadership style, and your purposes. After reviewing the Session Objectives, select the activities under each heading which will make up your first session together.

DARE TO RISK

> **SESSION OBJECTIVES**
>
> ✓ To get acquainted with one another by sharing how we see ourselves as risk-takers.
> ✓ To get an overview of the series.
> ✓ To become familiar with Matthew 14:22-33 as the basis and framework for the eight sessions.
> ✓ To challenge ourselves to follow a risk-taking model from the story in Matthew 14.

GETTING ACQUAINTED   20–25 minutes

The more time group members spend sharing their lives and experiences, the sooner they will bond into community. If your group is not well acquainted, take time to get to know one another's names before beginning this session. As part of the introductions, ask persons to tell the others what one or two words they would use to describe themselves and why (e.g., "I would choose the word 'intense' because whatever I do, I focus my energy and I'm really serious about it," or, "I would use the word 'hot-tempered' to describe myself because I tend to react in anger very easily to things that bother me," or, "I would say I'm 'friendly' because I enjoy meeting people and love getting to know even strangers").

Pocket Principle

1 It is often helpful to model the type of response you would like group members to give. By going first, you indicate such things as the amount of detail, depth, or brevity you're looking for. You also give others time to think about their response.

Optional—Why I'm Here

Ask group members to introduce themselves and in one or two sentences tell the others a primary reason they decided to become part of this small group.

Before continuing, give a brief overview of the series, so that people know clearly the content and purpose of the small

LEADER'S GUIDE

group. Use the Table of Contents and Comfort Zone or Twilight Zone to guide your comments.

Risky or Risk-free?
Guide the group through Risky or Risk-free, giving ample time to check the boxes that apply. Let group members know that this exercise is a quick way to help them assess their own risk-taking behavior. When everyone has finished the exercise, ask group members to share their responses. Go question by question, helping the group to discover how some persons are more cautious, while others tend to be more daring. Discuss how personalities affect risk-taking behavior.

If time permits and you feel it is appropriate, spend more time on question 6 of the exercise. This will give you and the others insight about any apprehension people may have about being part of the group. As you explore what makes people feel like their participation in the group is in any way risky, you can be more sensitive to individuals and the concerns they express. (You may prefer to address these apprehensions at the close of the session. See Optional—Wrestling with Risk.)

Pocket Principle

2 During the first meeting it is especially important that every person speak up at least once. Call on quiet or silent members to respond to a question when an answer is based on their personal experience or you know that they have a response to give.

GAINING INSIGHT   30–35 minutes

Real-life Risk
As a way to introduce the Scripture passage, ask a few people to share their responses to the following question: "What is one risk you took recently, and what was the outcome?"

Optional—Our Security Blankets
Like the Peanuts character, Linus, we all have our security blankets. Ask each person to share his or her response to the

75

following question: **What things or persons give you a sense of security? Why?** (e.g., family, money, relationship with God, friends, health, job)

Scripture Study
The Scripture text which undergirds *Dare to Risk* is Matthew 14:22-33. Role playing is one way to help people to interact with the material.

Select two expressive persons to play the parts of Jesus and Peter. Ask someone who reads well to be the narrator. The remaining persons will all be disciples. Give the group a few minutes to familiarize themselves with the material. Encourage them to use their imaginations and really pretend that they are experiencing the story themselves. Clear enough space in the room so that they may actually act out their parts using their bodies as well as their voices.

Pocket Principle

3 **Learning happens more easily when more than one sense is involved in the learning process. Role playing helps people remember because it involves hearing, seeing, and bodily movement.**

Set the scene. Prior to role playing, give the following background to put the passage in context:
1. Jesus had already chosen His disciples and was training them.
2. He had been healing and ministering around the Sea of Galilee.
3. This incident occurs right after the miracle of the feeding of the five thousand. Evidently, this miracle of feeding so impresses the people that they want Jesus to become their king.
4. In response, Jesus tells His disciples to get into their boat and sail to the other side of the lake, while He goes up to a mountain to pray.
5. The story makes reference to the fourth watch of the night. According to the Romans, the night was divided into four time periods. The fourth watch was from 3:00 A.M. to 6:00 A.M.

LEADER'S GUIDE

After setting the scene with the above information, role play the story in your group. When the role play concludes, ask the following questions:

❑ **What did you notice or learn about the disciples in the story?** (They got scared; at least they were in the boat, having obeyed the instructions Jesus gave them while on shore; their faith grew through the experience; people responded differently to the same event.)

❑ **What did you notice or learn about Peter?** (He was a little impulsive and tended to leap before he looked; he had enough faith to trust Jesus with his life; he got distracted by the wind.)

❑ **What did you notice or learn about Jesus?** (He responded to Peter's initiative; He still saved Peter, rescued him, even when he doubted; Jesus has power and control over everything; He is able to help us do what He asks us to do.)

❑ **As you look at this passage, what is God saying to you about your own risk-taking behavior?** (It may have something to do with one's family, spiritual walk, plans, a ministry responsibility, job, or a relationship: "I tend to be overly cautious"; "I dare to risk a lot"; "I think I trust God more than I thought"; "I'm a chicken at heart"; etc.)

GROWING BY DOING   15–20 minutes

Making Connections
Instruct group members to individually review the Matthew passage again and decide which person in the story they identify with most closely and why. Allow time for personal reflection on the questions, then form pairs to share responses. If appropriate, encourage partners to pray for each other after their discussion.

Optional—Wrestling with Risk
Using responses to question number 6 of Risky or Risk-free, have group members share in what ways they each feel their

DARE TO RISK

participation in this small group is risky for them. Ask: **What specific fears or kinds of apprehension do you feel as you think about the topic and developing relationships with others in this group?**

GOING THE SECOND MILE   5–10 minutes

As a way to keep the topic of risk-taking in their minds, ask group members to take note of how they respond to taking risks as they come up during the week. Tell them to come prepared next time to share their experiences with one another.

GROWING AS A LEADER

Like other kinds of leaders, small group leaders are made, not born. One way to develop and improve your skills is to take a little time after each session to assess how you did. The following questions are intended to help you evaluate your first meeting and to see in what ways you are taking risks as the leader of your small group.

Personal assessment
- ❏ In what ways did I feel comfortable leading the group during the first meeting?

- ❏ In what ways did I feel I was out of my comfort zone? What was the circumstance? What did I do?

- ❏ Would I do anything differently next time? What?

TWO

Peter's "Out-of-the-Boat" Experience

"Control" is an important word to most of us. We like control in our choices, our relationships, our careers, just about all areas of our lives. But when we take risks, we lose a degree of control. Unknowns enter into the picture. Things become uncertain. We're forced to exercise more faith.

The need for control is only one reason we often shy away from risk-taking. In this second session we'll explore the things that prevent us from taking risks. We'll look a little more closely at Matthew 14:22-33 and try to hear what Jesus is saying personally to each of us.

As the group leader of this small group experience, you can choose which learning activities will best fit your group, your style of leadership, and your purposes. After reviewing the Session Objectives, select the activities under each heading that you think will be most appropriate for your group.

DARE TO RISK

> **SESSION OBJECTIVES**
>
> ✓ To gain insight on how Jesus invites each of us to take risks in faith, using the example of Peter getting out of the boat to walk on water.
> ✓ To identify fears and obstacles associated with getting "out of the boat."
> ✓ To enhance our receptivity toward taking risks in the Christian life.
> ✓ To identify specific fears and opportunities for risk-taking in our lives right now.
> ✓ To continue to build relationships with each other.

GETTING ACQUAINTED   20–25 minutes

Invite group members to share what they noticed about their risk-taking behavior the previous week. Ask: What risks did you come across last week? How did you respond to them?

Ask a group member to read aloud Developing Trust. Then go into the following activity.

Pocket Principle

1 When a particular learning exercise requires careful planning, make sure that you have a very clear idea of what you are going to do and how you will communicate instructions to others. It is helpful to write down the instructions, listing them by number. Try them out beforehand so that modifications can be made, if necessary. This avoids confusion and wasted time in the small group.

Walking by Faith

The purpose of this activity is to give group members the experience of walking by faith and not by sight, having to trust a guide to lead them. If you have four or fewer in your small group, each person can have a turn being blindfolded. If

80

LEADER'S GUIDE

there are five or more, select two or three volunteers to be blindfolded. Be sure to have a bandana to cover their eyes so that they cannot see at all.

After the volunteers are identified, select one guide for each person who will be blindfolded. Have the guide take the blindfolded person through different parts of the house or building on a course you have predetermined. If your meeting space allows it, use more than one room. Going outdoors can also be quite effective. Quickly meet with the guides to show them the course. The course should not be too long or complicated, but have a few obstacles like stairs and furniture to force the blindfolded person to pay close attention to his or her guide. (Not allowing the blindfolded volunteers to know the course beforehand also forces them to trust their guides.) Tell the guides that they can lead their blindfolded partners by the arm or hand as well as direct them by voice.

Take one pair at a time. You can instruct the others to keep silent and observe, or you can tell them to try to distract the blindfolded person so that he or she has difficulty following the leading or instruction of the guide.

After the exercise, debrief with the questions under Walking by Faith:

❑ **What was it like (or what do you think it was like) not being able to see and having to rely on others to guide you?** (Negative feelings might include fear, vulnerability, doubt, apprehension, caution, resistance, helplessness, dependency; positive feelings might include trust, comfort, hope, confidence, excitement, enjoyment, security, faith, etc.)

❑ **What, if anything, hindered you from trusting your guide?** (Not knowing him or her well enough, my inability to depend on others, my need to stay in control, etc.)

❑ **What hinders you personally from trusting God completely?** (Inability to fully trust His promises, not knowing Him well enough, wanting control of my life, not believing in His trustworthiness, fear of being left out on a limb, etc.)

DARE TO RISK

Optional—Abbreviated Faith Walk
If your group is large or you think that the full faith walk activity will take too much time, you may want to have only two people go through it and use their experience as representative of the rest of the group. You can still use the discussion questions. Or, if no one wants to risk volunteering, you may allow group members to imagine what it would be like to be blindfolded and led around by someone else. Obviously, this is far less effective but workable. It also tells you something about the degree of risk-taking in your group!

Pocket Principle

> **2** People open up with people they like, trust, and know. This makes for better discussions. While activities during the sessions are meant to foster a sense of community, think about providing opportunities for people to interact with one another outside the small group context (e.g., potluck, picnic, taking in a movie together, etc.).

GAINING INSIGHT   30–35 minutes

A Man Called Peter
Ask a few group members to read aloud Matthew 14:22-33. As you read the text together, encourage the group to think about Peter's actions and attitudes and how similar or different they are from their own.

Pocket Principle

> **3** To hold people's attention while reading aloud a Scripture that is longer than six or eight verses, ask group members to take turns reading a few verses each. Know beforehand how you plan to divide up the passages, using the given paragraph divisions or natural units of thought. Do not break up verses that are incomplete sentences—doing so makes the content difficult to follow.

LEADER'S GUIDE

After reading the text, follow the material outlined and discuss the questions included.

❑ **What do you think Peter's motives were when he made this statement?** (Perhaps he wanted to show off, test his own faith, seek a proof from Jesus, go to where the Lord was, etc.)

❑ **When have you encountered a situation or circumstance where you heard Jesus say, "Come!" and you had to decide to obey or not to obey?** (Career move, change in geographical location, new ministry responsibility, etc.)

❑ **What are some winds and waves that come to people, and which of these have you experienced personally?** (Lack of finances, fear of failure, a sense of inadequacy, relational conflicts, lack of encouragement or support, a feeling of being alone or lonely, institutional barriers, criticism by others, etc.)

❑ **If you were to interview Peter, how do you think he would respond to this question: "What lessons did you learn about Jesus and being obedient in risk-taking?"** (When we start drowning, we can call out to the Lord for help, and He comes to our rescue, even when we doubt and get distracted; we can take risks because we know God rescues; we can be obedient even when it feels like God is asking us to do the impossible, because He won't let us drown; the One who calls us out of the boat has the power to keep us afloat; He doesn't ask us to do anything He won't empower us to do.)

❑ **What effect do you think Peter's risk-taking had on the lives of others?** (Helped the disciples to understand more of who Jesus is because they saw His power and care demonstrated. Peter's act led to worship of the Son of God.)

GROWING BY DOING 15–20 minutes

Here is the time for group members to more fully apply what they have learned in this session. The questions are intended

DARE TO RISK

to help people to personalize Jesus' words to Peter and encourage them to call out to Him where they feel they're drowning in life.

If you are short on time, ask group members to select one of the three questions and share their response to it. If people all address the same question, encourage them to respond to one of the other two. The variety will add insight.

Pocket Principle

4 **Some group members may want to sit on the floor. Encourage them to sit in chairs or on the couch so that everyone is at equal eye level. Easy eye contact usually leads to better discussions.**

GOING THE SECOND MILE   5–10 minutes

Ask group members to journal their thoughts in response to each of the questions in Growing by Doing. Encourage them to pray about becoming more open to risk-taking as God assures them of His power and provision in their lives.

GROWING AS A LEADER

A number of factors affect good discussions. Leadership and communication skills are important, but these other factors also contribute to the quality of a small group discussion:

Relationships
What kinds of opportunities am I providing to help people get to know each other?

Content
What shows me that the kinds of activities I'm selecting for the group are appropriate for who we are and where we are in life?

Physical Environment
What tells me that the people feel comfortable and welcome in the group?

- ❏ Seating arrangements—How are people seated? Is everyone at the same level of eye contact so they sense mutuality? Do we form a complete circle with our chairs, indicating a sense of closeness and unity?

- ❏ Furniture—Do lamps block anyone's view of another person? Does a coffee table in the middle of the room create an obstacle to easy communication? What pieces of furniture help or hinder the communication process or our sense of closeness?

- ❏ Lighting—Can everyone see to read the material and see one another's faces clearly? Since lighting sets a mood, what kind of mood are we creating?

- ❏ Temperature—Am I aware of anything that indicates to me that the temperature of the room is affecting a person's concentration or ability to participate (e.g., fanning themselves, shivering, putting on their coats, etc.)?

- ❏ Auditory and visual distractions—Am I aware of any auditory and visual distractions which make it difficult for people to concentrate? Are telephones ringing, dogs barking, children crying, or clocks ticking too loudly? What about distracting magazines in the room, cars driving by the open window, or people passing through the meeting room? Which distractions am I able to remove?

THREE

Getting Out of the Boat with Our Material Needs

The security we place in material possessions is probably one of the biggest obstacles to wholeheartedly trusting God. Jesus knew of our difficulty in this area. In His ministry He made reference to money and materialism more times than any other topic, except for the kingdom of God.

This third session looks at how trusting in material possessions hinders Christians from getting out of the boat, especially when the consequence of obedience may be financial. It focuses on both the difficulty to trust God for our material needs and our tendency to overvalue the things we do possess. We get stuck in the boat for two reasons: We don't want to risk letting go of the things we have, and we don't trust that if we do get out onto the water, God will give us the material things we need to keep us afloat.

As group leader, you have the option to select which elements best fit your group, your style of leadership, and your purposes. After you examine the Session Objectives, choose the activities which seem most appropriate for your group.

LEADER'S GUIDE

SESSION OBJECTIVES

✓ To assess to what extent we derive security from our ability to provide for our own material needs.
✓ To gain insight into the relationship between anxiety and trusting God with one's material needs and possessions.
✓ To identify the obstacles that hinder us from trusting God with our finances and material possessions.
✓ To begin to take concrete steps toward taking more risks in faith and obedience in the area of material possessions and needs.

GETTING ACQUAINTED   20–25 minutes

Ask a group member to read aloud Possessions. Then choose one or more of the following activities to help people get to know each other better and as an introduction to the topic of risk-taking and our material needs and possessions.

Pocket Principle

1 **When deciding on which activities to use with a group, think about specific characteristics, such as age, individual and group needs, degree of intimacy with one another, identified objectives, and group members' personalities. Try to imagine beforehand how others might respond to each activity. Taking time to select the appropriate introductory activity is especially important because it sets the tone and focus for the entire meeting.**

Anxiety Levels

This activity addresses our inability to trust God completely for our material needs. It touches on how much a person relies on his or her own ability to make ends meet. After

87

each group member completes the exercise, compare and discuss responses. Affirm those with low scores, telling them that the group has much to learn from them. Assure those with higher scores that we are all people in process and that the fact they are willing to grapple with this difficult area is commendable. They are already showing a willingness to take a risk and be open to change. Mention that the Scripture text chosen for this session is intended to help everyone to rethink how important material things are to us and who or in what we tend to put our trust.

Necessity or Luxury?
Very often part of the reason we can't trust God to meet our needs is because we confuse wants and needs. A false understanding of what constitute the necessities of life makes our risk-taking in this area of material needs more difficult. By identifying how we differentiate luxuries and necessities, we are able to see why it is difficult for us to trust God to provide for our needs. The longer a person's list of necessities, the more he or she must trust God for!

After the group completes the chart, discuss their reactions and feelings to it. Ask: What did you discover about yourself or your views of necessities and luxuries? How does this view affect your ability to trust God with your material needs and possessions?

Optional—A Big Winner
Read the following to the group and discuss the question at the end. Encourage them to be as honest as possible, assuring them that the intention is not to judge or criticize their use of money, but to dream and be imaginative.

Imagine! You have just been notified that you are the $5 million winner of this year's Reader's Digest Sweepstakes. All of your friends and family are, of course, excited. They are also curious to know what you are going to do with all the money. What will you tell them? Be specific.

Optional—Choosing What to Take
Read the following to the group and discuss the question at the end.

LEADER'S GUIDE

Imagine that you are an emigrant or political refugee who is leaving your country. You can take only what you can carry with you. You'll be crossing the border on foot, so you have to think about traveling light. What would you take with you?

Optional — Wiped Out
Read the following to the group and discuss the questions at the end.

In recent years, the news has carried a number of stories about natural disasters. Tornadoes, earthquakes, floods, and fires have been bringing devastation and death to persons and their property. Some people also get wiped out financially from business losses, medical expenses, or other personal crises. Have you ever experienced severe material or financial loss? How did you react? If you haven't had this kind of experience, how do you think you would feel, and what would you do?

Pocket Principle

2 One way to help control any member from dominating a discussion is to sit right next to him or her. Lack of eye contact with you as the leader makes it more difficult for that person to speak up. Likewise, by positioning yourself opposite more quiet members so that you have the greatest eye contact with them, you encourage them to participate more.

GAINING INSIGHT   30–35 minutes

A Choice and a Promise

Matthew 6:24-34 addresses the question of where we put our trust and offers assurance to those who are anxious about their material needs. The passage highlights the relationship between anxiety and trust in God.

Ask one person to read Matthew 6:24, a second person to read Matthew 6:25-27, and a third person, Matthew 6:28-34.

DARE TO RISK

Then lead a discussion based on the questions provided. The notes which follow are intended to help you facilitate the discussion.

Note: In verse 24, the term *Money* means material possessions in general, not a vast amount of capital. It more represents the principle of materialism and, in this sense, can claim a person's loyalty or allegiance. A person becomes a slave to money and possessions when he doesn't use them to serve God. Jesus is not saying that material possessions in and of themselves are bad, but that we must not substitute them for God.

❑ **What do you think Jesus meant when He said, "You cannot serve God and Money"?** (It's not possible to love God and love money at the same time; a Christian can't be materialistic and follow God wholeheartedly; to be materialistic and a Christian is an oxymoron, or at least should be; God must come first in your life; Christians should follow God, not seek after material gain; obedience to God must come before any material considerations; etc.)

❑ **Have you made a conscious, specific choice to serve, love, and be devoted to God? How does that decision show itself in your daily life?** (I haven't really made a deliberate choice; I made a choice ten years ago when . . . ; No, and that's why I'm still very materialistic; etc.)

❑ **Right now, what hinders you from wholeheartedly trusting God to meet all your material needs?** (I don't really believe He'll come through for me if I experience financial need; I think that part of being a responsible Christian is to keep a sizable savings account; I feel like God has failed me in the past; etc.)

❑ **Right now, what hinders you from letting go of and trusting God with your material possessions?** (I'm afraid He'll ask me to give up a lot of them; I'm afraid that if I'm obedient I might end up poor; I have a feeling I won't be able to buy the things I want; I like having control over my possessions; I gain a sense of security from

LEADER'S GUIDE

what I own; I mistakenly equate obedience with poverty; etc.)

NOTE: In verse 32, the reference to "pagans" is to people who do not know God. Understandably, they place value in material possessions and are concerned about material things because they do not know the Heavenly Father who takes care of all His children. Christians, however, do. And even then, we fret and worry.

❏ **What do you think it means to seek first the kingdom of God and His righteousness?** (To seek to be obedient and bring every aspect of my life under the lordship of Christ; to allow God to rule over everything in my life; to put God first in everything; to be obedient at all costs; give God total control; make Jesus' mission my own; etc.)

NOTE: Many Jews in Jesus' day were expecting God to send a messiah ("anointed one") who would establish the kingdom of God as a political and geographical entity in which Israel would be independent and free of any foreign domination and oppression. However, when Jesus came announcing the kingdom of God, He was not referring to an earthly realm. Rather, the kingdom of God is the rule, reign, and power of God over people's lives and in their hearts. It is a spiritual reality for those who surrender their wills to God the King, through Jesus Christ. Jesus' mission was to inaugurate that rule of God on earth by demonstrating God's presence and power through healing the sick, casting out demons, and forgiving sins.

Jesus and many Jews, especially the Pharisees, also differed in their understanding of the term *righteousness*. The Pharisees were devout Jews who believed that ritual purity and strict adherence to the Old Testament law was what it meant to be righteous and obedient to God. This is why they could not understand why Jesus ate with tax collectors and sinners. Such people were "unclean" and in open defiance of the law. (See Matthew 9:9-12.)

For Jesus, righteousness had to do with conformity to the will of God in acts of mercy, goodness, and kindness. Ritual purity was less important than ethical behavior toward a fellow hu-

91

DARE TO RISK

man being. He did not disregard the law; He taught and lived out the true spirit of the law (Matthew 5:17-20). Righteousness is living as Jesus lived. (See Mark 7:1-23; Matthew 12:1-14.) It is the result of a relationship with Him.

In light of this understanding of the kingdom of God and righteousness, to seek God's kingdom first is to put God first in our lives. To seek God's righteousness is to be committed to Jesus in discipleship that demonstrates behavior, actions, and character consistent with His life and teaching.

- ❏ **What does God's promise of assurance (v. 33) mean to you?** (God knows what I need; all the things I need will be given to me; He is a God of unlimited resources; He cares about me more than birds and lilies; etc.)

- ❏ **If you have not already done so, what will it take to get you to let go of your possessions and get out of the boat with your material needs? Be specific.** (A crisis; a miracle; a kick in the pants; someone to hold me accountable; a direct encounter with God; an increase in faith; a stronger relationship with God; etc.)

Pocket Principle

3 Silence in a group can feel uncomfortable. Sometimes it results when people do not understand a question you ask. If this is the case, simply ask if they need the question repeated, and rephrase it for clarification. Other times, silence results when you ask questions which require personal application rather than simple fact or observation; people need time to reflect on their responses. Be patient; wait at least 15–20 seconds before speaking again, either to restate the question, ask someone to share, or offer your own response.

LEADER'S GUIDE

GROWING BY DOING 15–20 minutes

Direct people into groups of three and ask them to respond to the question, "What is one thing that I can do this week to demonstrate my willingness to trust God with my possessions and get out of the boat with my material needs?" It may be asking God to help them let go of a materialistic attitude, or giving away clothes, furniture, or appliances they really do not need. It may mean beginning to tithe regularly, or giving money away where they know it's needed. If members of the group seem stuck for ideas, offer these as suggestions. Encourage them to refer back to the group discussion and what they learned.

Pocket Principle

4 **When married couples are in your group, be sure that they are not always in the same grouping when you break up into smaller units. Often when they are separated, each partner tends to feel freer to share, and others are able to more easily get to know them as individuals.**

Optional—Putting God First

Direct people into pairs or groups of three and ask them to respond to these questions:

❑ In what ways do your finances and material possessions get in the way of your relationship with God?

❑ What must you do to give the Lord more control over these things?

❑ How can this small group help you?

GOING THE SECOND MILE 5–10 minutes

Try to make sure that each person commits to doing one thing that concretely demonstrates a willingness to be more

93

DARE TO RISK

open to taking risks in the area of material things. Then encourage everyone to memorize Hebrews 13:5-6, as a way to keep God's promise to them in their minds and hearts.

Optional — Contentment
Ask group members to meditate during the week on Philippians 4:10-13 and Paul's ability to be content in whatever circumstances he found himself, with or without material comfort or possessions.

GROWING AS A LEADER

Leading discussions requires specific skills. But who we are as people, along with our attitudes, is also important. The following characteristics contribute positively to a small group leader's effectiveness.

- ❑ Relaxed: In what ways do I communicate to others that I am relaxed and comfortable and help them to feel the same?

- ❑ Accepting: How judgmental am I when people share thoughts and feelings that are different from mine?

- ❑ Affirming: In what genuine and sincere ways do I communicate to each person how special he or she is?

- ❑ Humorous: What do I do to contribute laughter and a sense of levity to the group?

- ❑ Open: When and to what extent have I expressed some of my deeper thoughts and feelings to help our group grow in intimacy and trust?

- ❑ Honest: When and to what extent have I shared my thoughts and feelings even when it meant being vulnerable or experiencing potential conflict with others?

FOUR

Getting Out of the Boat with Our Careers

Our society is big on measuring success by what people do and how much money they make. Many choose a career or occupation based on its perceived status and anticipated income rather than using interest or sense of calling as the primary criterion. Our desire to be successful in the world's eyes often creates static that interferes with hearing God's will for our lives. And because our self-worth tends to be tied to our social and economic status and the recognition we receive from it, we find it difficult to take risks with our careers. Many of us would rather be known as doctors, lawyers, engineers, and accountants than as "fools for Christ" (1 Corinthians 1:18-30; 4:10-13). Our primary identity is wrapped up in our jobs and not as servants in the kingdom of God.

In this fourth session, we will look at our careers in light of our relationship to God and our risk-taking behavior in this area. We will examine the extent to which our jobs and careers define who we are and how they might hinder us from being totally available to God for His purposes.

As group leader, you have the option to select which elements best fit your group, your style of leadership, and your

DARE TO RISK

purposes. After you review the Session Objectives, choose the activities that seem most appropriate for your group.

SESSION OBJECTIVES

✓ To discover to what extent our careers define our identities.
✓ To reflect on what happened when Jesus called Peter and others to leave their careers to follow Him.
✓ To assess in what ways our careers can hinder our obedience to God and taking risks in faith.
✓ To give God more control over our career and job choices, even if it feels risky.

GETTING ACQUAINTED   20–25 minutes

Follow up on the previous meeting's Going the Second Mile assignment. Ask a few members to share how they demonstrated their willingness to get out of the boat with their material needs.

Pocket Principle

1 **When addressing a question to someone, let your physical posture and facial gestures communicate interest in what the other is saying. A slight leaning toward the person without arms crossed, with positive eye contact, conveys a readiness to hear and indicates that what is said is valuable to the group.**

Introduce the topic for this session and ask a group member to read aloud "What Do You Do?"

Work and Me

Ask members to each share how they came to be in their career or current position and the extent to which they enjoy what they do for a living. Challenge them by asking: How hard would it be for you to give up what you do, and why?

Optional—Contemplating Career Moves

This exercise is intended to help individuals determine how much they place security in their jobs and derive a sense of identity, status, and fulfillment from them. It brings out the degree to which each person places his or her job under the lordship of Jesus Christ and is willing to let go of it if asked.

While this activity is under the Getting Acquainted heading, it is an individual exercise in which the primary focus is communication between God and the group member.

In preparation for the activity, write an individual letter to each person in the group. Place it in an envelope, seal it, and write the person's name on it. Make it as personal as you can.

Inside, write the letter as you would any other. Include the date, the person's name, and a closing, which should be signed, "Your Heavenly Father," or, "God." In the body of the letter, use the questions which appear in the following sample letters. If appropriate for your group, simply copy the sample letters, changing the dates and names.

Here are two sample letters:

May 24th

Dear Sharon,

I have a new ministry assignment for you. It requires quitting your present job and devoting yourself full-time to missionary work in Haiti. Would you be willing to consider it? What would it take for you to say yes to Me? What are your greatest fears about saying yes? How does this possible career change affect your identity and your sense of self-worth? How ready are you to get out of the boat and walk on water as you hear Me say, "Come"?

Sharon, you know that I love you, and I will provide for all your needs. But I also know how scary it can feel taking such a risk in faith. So please write back and share your thoughts with Me.

In My grace and love,

DARE TO RISK

May 24th

Dear Rob,

I have a new ministry assignment for you. You know that big promotion you were offered with a 15 percent increase in pay? Well, I have better plans for you. I do not want you to take the position. I know you think that it will help with all the household expenses, but it would require too much additional time on your part. Instead, I want you to use that time to witness to Me through your community service activities.

Would you be willing to consider it? What would it take for you to say yes to Me? What are your greatest fears about saying yes? How does My request affect how you think about your career, your identity, and sense of self-worth? How ready are you to get out of the boat and walk on water as you hear Me say, "Come"?

Rob, you know that I love you, and I will provide for all your needs. But I also know how scary it can feel taking risks and being obedient in faith. So please write back and share your thoughts with Me.

In My grace and love,

NOTE: For those who do not work outside the home, you can ask them to imagine what they do for the purposes of this exercise, or have them think back to a time when they were employed. For career moms or dads (those whose primary occupation is in the home raising children), you might have them think through to what extent their role as parents defines who they are relative to their identity in Christ.

Ask group members to write their responses on a separate piece of paper, then debrief with them. Ask: **What did you discover about yourself, your job, and your relationship with God?**

Pocket Principle

2 Some people need more prompting than others to share their thoughts and feelings. Nodding your head slightly when they do speak encourages them to continue. Brief comments such as, "Uh-huh," "Really?" "Tell us more," invite the speaker to continue without distracting him or her or changing the topic or focus of attention.

GAINING INSIGHT   30–35 minutes

From Fishermen to Followers
Matthew 4:18-22 gives the account of Jesus calling His first disciples, one of whom is Simon Peter, the same man who later walks on water. Jesus has just begun His public ministry and is seeking those who will become His followers. When He approaches the men mentioned in the text, it is not for the first time. Other Gospel accounts (e.g., John 1:35-42; Luke 5:3, 10) indicate that they might have had interaction with Jesus prior to this experience. However, Jesus' invitation to them to follow Him was probably the first time they received a definite call to discipleship and total commitment to His person and teaching.

Use the information given in this section to briefly introduce the Matthew passage. Ask one person to read the Scripture text, and then lead a discussion based on the questions in the book.

Pocket Principle

3 Extending is one communication technique to pursue a particular topic or line of thinking more fully. After a response has been offered in the discussion, ask questions such as, "What more can be said about this?" "Have we left anything out?" or "What else comes to your mind?"

DARE TO RISK

- ❑ **What type of career did Peter and his brother Andrew have?** (They made a living by fishing; they were fishermen.)

- ❑ **What did Jesus tell Peter and Andrew?** (He said, "Follow Me, and I will make you fishers of men.")

- ❑ **What do you think Jesus meant by, "Follow Me, and I will make you fishers of men"?** (He was asking them to become His disciples, telling them that they would learn how to "catch" people for the kingdom of God. They were to be evangelists, bringing people good news of salvation. Jesus was asking them to give up their careers to do something radically different. Their primary identity was no longer to be fishermen but to be followers of Jesus.)

- ❑ **What did this career move mean for Peter, Andrew, James, and John?** (Leaving a relatively secure living; embarking on the unknown; letting go of a steady source of income; learning a new "career"; taking on a new identity; etc.)

- ❑ **Knowing what you do from the New Testament, what was the outcome of the decision these fishermen made?** (They did fish for people; they followed Jesus; they became leaders of the early church; etc. They also died for the decision.)

- ❑ **If you had been at the Sea of Galilee with these fishermen, what feelings, fears, or obstacles would have hindered you from following Jesus when He called your name?** (Doubts about who Jesus really was; fear about leaving something familiar; not wanting to appear different from my peers; feelings of intimidation or inadequacy; etc.)

- ❑ **In what ways do you suppose Peter's clear decision to become a follower of Jesus at this point affected his ability later to get out of the boat and walk on water?** (His intentional choice to follow Jesus probably helped him when he faced decisions of obedience, like when Jesus called him out of the boat.)

LEADER'S GUIDE

GROWING BY DOING   15–20 minutes

Help people to personalize what they learned from the Scripture study by grouping them in pairs and asking them to share with one another their responses to these questions:

❑ **What is the primary source of your identity? To what extent does it come from being a follower of Jesus and how much does it come from your career, job, or occupation?** (I'd like to see myself first as a follower, but I know my primary identity is still as a mom; my primary identity is as a teacher, and it's not hard for me to separate what I do for a living from my Christian beliefs; etc.)

❑ **In what ways does your current career or job affect your obedience to God and taking risks in faith?** (My job gives me so much security, I would find it hard to think about taking risks with it, even if I knew it meant being obedient to God; I like my job a lot, and I'm afraid that if I tell God I'm open to quitting it, He might ask me to become a missionary in Africa; my job keeps me obedient and dependent on God because the environment is so hostile to the Gospel; I feel like staying in my job is being obedient and taking a risk; etc.)

❑ **With reference to your job or career, what attitude change or action is God asking you to make? How will you concretely respond to Him?** (God wants me to trust Him more; God has been asking me to quit my job for a while now, and I need to think seriously about being obedient; I need to look into my options for missionary service; I feel really good about where God has me, and I need to be more thankful that He's taking care of me; etc.)

Pocket Principle

4 Many times, things that a group member says in a discussion are not understood by those listening. As the leader you may need to seek clarification to clear up possible confusion or misunderstanding. To do this, ask questions such as, "Could you restate that?" "Do you mean...?"

DARE TO RISK

or, "Could you say a little more about what you mean?"

GOING THE SECOND MILE 5–10 minutes

Tell the group to find at least one person during the week who has made a significant career change based on God's calling and interview them regarding how they made the change and what their life has been like since. The interviewee may be a pastor, friend, or someone else they know or have heard of. It may even be a fellow group member. To help ensure follow-through, spend some time as a group talking about possible contacts and then ask each member to select a person.

Optional—Marketplace Minister
Encourage each person to meet with someone who clearly lives out his or her faith on the job in a secular environment and sees that job or responsibility primarily as a ministry on behalf of Christ to the world. Suggest that during the interview they ask these questions:

- What enables you to keep a firm identity in Christ when you have so many pressures that come from a secular work environment?
- What counsel can you give me as I seek to be obedient and take risks in faith in my career or job?

GROWING AS A LEADER

Comfort Zone Assessment
In session 1, under Growing as a Leader, you responded to questions about your comfort zone in leadership. Now that you have led four sessions of this group, write down your answers to the following questions, and then compare them to those in the first session.

- After four sessions, how much more comfortable am I as the leader of this group?

LEADER'S GUIDE

- ❏ How has my comfort zone changed since the first session?
- ❏ In what specific circumstances am I more comfortable?
- ❏ What things do I know how to do better?
- ❏ What specifically have I begun to do differently and more effectively as the leader?

FIVE

Getting Out of the Boat with Our Relationships

Relationships not only affect the decisions we make but, like our careers, they significantly impact our sense of identity. As Christians, our most important relationship should be with God, as His child and as a disciple of His Son Jesus Christ. But it's not that easy. The other significant relationships in our lives often make it difficult to put God first. When God asks us to do things that threaten the security we derive from the relationships we have with those we love, we find our loyalty and allegiance divided.

In this fifth session, we will look at the important relationships in our lives and how they affect us and our obedience to God. The focus is on putting Him first in our lives. We'll see how we gain true life and identity when we are willing to run the risk of losing our relationships in order to give the Lord our primary loyalty.

As group leader, you have the option to select which elements best fit your group, your style of leadership, and your purposes. After you examine the Session Objectives, choose the activities that seem most appropriate for your group.

LEADER'S GUIDE

SESSION OBJECTIVES

✓ To understand what it means to follow Jesus above all.
✓ To identify which of our relationships help and hinder our risk-taking in obedience to God.
✓ To celebrate the positive aspects of gaining our identity from Jesus, not from our human relationships.
✓ To support one another in letting go of the relationships which prevent us from "getting out of the boat" to obey God.

GETTING ACQUAINTED   20–25 minutes

Ask one person to read Significant Others. Then move into the following activity.

Ship and Shore

The purpose of this exercise is to help people to identify the significant people in their lives and the roles they play in helping or hindering them from being obedient to God.

After group members have written their lists and marked them according to the instructions, ask: **In what ways do the people you listed seem to help you or hinder you from "walking on water"?**

Pocket Principle

1 **Preparation is key to effective leading. This means that you should not only have your content well outlined, but you should pay attention to even seemingly minor details. If an activity calls for paper and pens/pencils, make sure that you have them available for anyone who has forgotten theirs. Being prepared at this level prevents wasting time and makes the session flow more smoothly.**

105

Optional — Under the Influence
This exercise is intended to help people realize how much other people in their lives have had a significant influence in shaping who they are and what they do. Ask group members to volunteer to respond to this question: Who is one person in your life that has exerted tremendous influence over you, and how does their influence show itself in who you are today?

Optional — Missing Persons
This activity may be helpful if you have a number of persons in your group who are not content with their current relationships and are looking for new ones of significance. This may be the case with single people who have a strong desire to be married or remarried or those who yearn for intimate friendships.

Tell the group that in life we experience a variety of relationships. Some are between friends, within families, with members of the opposite sex. Ask them: **What is one relationship you would like to have in your life but currently don't have, and how does not having it affect your relationship with God?**

Optional — Choosing and Losing
This exercise is intended to help group members share with one another how their relationship with God brought conflict into relationships with others they love. Ask them to think of a situation in which being obedient to God meant potentially or actually losing a relationship they held dearly. Ask a few members to share the circumstances, the outcome, and what they learned from it.

If people have difficulty thinking of something, give examples: a decision to accept Christ meant rejecting the religion of one's parents; a call into full-time ministry jeopardized one's relationship with an older brother; an act of obedience meant relocating and jeopardizing a relationship with a girlfriend; a call to the mission field in retirement was costly to the relationship with one's children; being obedient to follow the commands of Christ in the workplace threatened one's relationship with a supervisor.

LEADER'S GUIDE

Pocket Principle

2 Very often people speak in generalities. Rather than saying, "I think," or "I feel," they say, "Some people think...." "Others I know feel...." Don't be afraid to tell the group to try to share their own personal feelings. Doing so builds trust and deepens the level of communication in the group.

Who's Number One?
Give group members only a few minutes to rate their relationships and then ask two or three people to volunteer their responses to the question which accompanies the exercise. This activity provides a natural lead-in to the Scripture Study.

GAINING INSIGHT   25–30 minutes

Cost of Discipleship
Explain that this session's Scripture Study is about putting our relationships in perspective and making them secondary to our primary relationship to Christ. Very often relationships prevent us from taking risks in faith because we place higher priority on our relationships with other people than being obedient to God. The text from Matthew 10:37-39 challenges us to get out of the boat with our relationships and gives us the assurance that when we do, we gain far more than we ever lose.

Ask one person to read the introduction and a second person the text of Matthew 10:37-39. Then discuss the following questions.

Pocket Principle

3 Paraphrasing is a helpful communication technique to make sure that what is heard is the meaning the speaker intended. It involves a restatement of what is said—not simply repeating verbatim the words, but getting at the meaning

DARE TO RISK

and feelings conveyed. Examples of paraphrasing include statements that begin with, "You seem to be saying...," "I sense you mean...," "You've expressed the idea that...," "What you want is...," "What you're feeling is...," etc.

☐ **What do you think Jesus meant when He said that those loving father, mother, son, or daughter more than Him are not worthy of Him?** (A person's relationship with Christ is to come first in one's life; family loyalties are secondary to commitment to Christ; unless we choose to obey and love God above all else and everyone else, we have no business calling ourselves disciples; belonging to Christ means submitting former sources of belonging to His lordship; etc.)

☐ **Look again at how you rated your relationships in importance and priority. What is affirming or convicting about your ratings? What place does God have in your life right now? How do you feel about it?** (E.g., my mother's influence is much too strong over me. I rated God as higher in priority than I would have a year ago, so I must be moving in the right direction. I didn't realize how much I allow my best friend to affect my decisions and actions. I placed God first, but I know He's not there 100 percent of the time.)

☐ **What do you think it means to take up the cross and follow Jesus today?** (The cross represents total commitment. It means dying to the things that define who you are. We are to die to ourselves. It means choosing the way of suffering. It's voluntarily letting go of all the things which distract us from following God. It's choosing to identify with Jesus and His mission in the world. Taking up the cross indicates our willingness to belong to God.)

Pocket Principle

4 Opinion-seeking or information-seeking is a form of question-asking that draws people into a discussion. It involves directly addressing someone with a question or

LEADER'S GUIDE

comment such as, "John, what do you think (feel or know) about . . . ?" "Bev, I'd be interested in your opinion on . . . ." Wayne, what do you notice about . . . ?"

❑ **How are we to understand the paradox that one who finds his life will lose it, and one who loses his life for Jesus' sake will find it?** (Those who try to keep their lives for themselves will lose them, and those who give their lives to Jesus Christ will find the true meaning and purpose of their lives. It's in giving God control of your life that you end up knowing what to do with it.)

❑ **How have you found this paradox to be true in your own life?** (E.g., the more I let God control my life, the more rewarding and fulfilling it is. The more I try to hold on and take charge of my life, the more I feel like it's slipping away from me. When I decided to trust God with my career decision, He gave me a wonderful job that I didn't even know existed.)

GROWING BY DOING   20–25 minutes

Ask someone to read aloud the questions given, and then divide into groups of three. Tell the groups how much time they have for the discussion, and remind them to leave time at the end to pray for one another. At least five minutes before moving into the Going the Second Mile section, indicate to the groups that they should be praying together, if they are not already doing so.

Optional—Give and Take
Total commitment to Christ involves two actions on our part: giving up of our lives to God and taking up our cross. Our relationships are part of that giving up process. Part of taking up our cross means to let go of those we love. When we take hold of the cross, we are to let go of those we hold close to us and who have a hold on us.

This activity gives group members the opportunity to express their giving up and taking up symbolically. Ask them to write on slips of paper the names of those who hinder them from

DARE TO RISK

being more obedient to God in risk-taking and faith. Have them place the slips of paper in a container as an expression of their desire and commitment to live out their primary allegiance to God and put their relationship with Him first in their lives. For added effect, you may want to put all the slips of paper in an ashtray and burn them as a group.

As a way to demonstrate taking up the cross, spend time in conversational prayer, allowing group members to express their commitment to the way of the cross and following Jesus. This activity could also be used with reference to giving up of possessions, career, dreams, painful memories, etc.

Optional—Eureka! I Found It!
If many in your group are already risk-takers in faith and obedience, this question may be more appropriate: In what ways have you personally already found your life as you have chosen to lose it for Christ's sake? After discussing their responses, encourage them to lift up praises and prayers of thanksgiving for the ways they can personally bear testimony to the truth of God's Word.

GOING THE SECOND MILE   5–10 minutes

This activity demonstrates how many people recorded in the Bible risked their human relationships to obey God. It is meant to encourage group members to do the same. You may want to provide a few examples: Abraham risked his son Isaac, willing to make of him a sacrifice; Jonathan risked his relationship with his father Saul to protect David; Mary risked her relationship with her family and fiancé Joseph through the Virgin Birth; etc.

Be sensitive to those group members who may feel inadequate for this assignment because of their limited knowledge of Scripture. You may wish to assign them a character and tell them the appropriate passages to look up, or prepare a list of characters and passages from which to choose.

GROWING AS A LEADER

Communication skills are critical to leading good discussions. The Pocket Principles given in session 4 and this session are intended to increase your skills in this area. How well are you practicing them?

- ❑ Attending: What did I do with my face, body, and gestures to indicate interest in what was being said? What comments did I make to encourage the speaker to continue sharing thoughts or feelings? What can I do to improve my effectiveness?

- ❑ Clarification: In what specific instances did I seek to clarify a speaker's thoughts, ideas, or feelings? How did I do this, and what was the outcome? What would I do differently next time?

- ❑ Extending: How often and in what instances did I use this listening technique? What was the outcome? Was my judgment appropriate? How can I improve my skill in this area?

SIX

Getting Out of the Boat with Our Convictions

For many Christians, the commands of Scripture and the ministry of Jesus to the poor and downcast of society create uneasiness and guilt. The thought of doing such things as visiting prisoners, feeding the hungry, and being an advocate for the oppressed are way out of the comfort zones of most of us.

Generally, our problem is not one of ignorance or lack of conviction, but one of apprehension or resistance. We know what the Bible says. We hear the Lord challenging us to move further out of our safe places to take risks in obedience to Him. We don't need more guilt heaped on us but rather need help to discover the positive steps we can take to live out our convictions in the world. In this session, we'll try to move in the direction of such discovery.

As group leader, you have the option to select which elements best fit your group, your style of leadership, and your purposes. After you examine the Session Objectives, choose the activities that seem the most appropriate for your group.

LEADER'S GUIDE

SESSION OBJECTIVES

✓ To identify our feelings about being involved in ministering to the needs of the poor and oppressed.
✓ To encourage those seeking to respond to God's concern for the poor and oppressed.
✓ To select and engage in a social action activity which moves us out of our comfort zones.
✓ To commit to praying about the needs of our community and world and our personal involvement in social concerns.

GETTING ACQUAINTED   20–25 minutes

Begin this session by following up with the Going the Second Mile assignment from last time. Ask two people to share their homework about the Bible character they chose who risked a significant relationship to be obedient to God.

First Things First?
This activity is intended to help people articulate their perspective on the place of social and political action in the Christian life. If you choose to use this exercise, conduct it at the beginning of the meeting, right after covering the Second Mile homework and before you read On Uneasy Street. This will give people greater permission to express a variety of opinions about the relationship between Christian convictions and social action.

On Uneasy Street
Ask someone to read On Uneasy Street. Explain that, just as getting out of the boat with our relationships can jeopardize them, getting out of the boat with our convictions is potentially costly as well. But God gives us certain commands which we are to follow, and this session we will seek to help one another take steps to live them out.

Personal Assessment
Use the questions given to help group members explore their feelings about ministry to their community and world and to

DARE TO RISK

recall their own experiences in this area. Define ministry as any service or act done in the name of Jesus Christ to meet the needs of others.

GAINING INSIGHT   30–35 minutes

Doers of the Word
Ask someone to read Doers of the Word. Then tell the group to take a few minutes to read James 2:14-17 silently.

After everyone has read the passage, conduct a brief discussion about how they react to this passage and others like it. This discussion is simply to help people begin verbalizing their feelings about the topic. Do not go into too much detail, and be sure to focus primarily on what people feel, not what they think.

Optional—Expanded Doers of the Word
If you have Bibles available, invite group members to read Matthew 25:31-46 silently before responding to the questions in Doers of the Word.

The Miracle of Multiplication
Mark 8:1-10 focuses on the feeding of the 4,000. In Mark's Gospel, this miracle takes place in the region of the Decapolis, somewhat southeast of the Sea of Galilee. The region was characterized by high Greek culture. It is believed that both Gentiles and Jews made up the 4,000. Just as the compassion of Jesus moved Him to teach the crowds and feed the 5,000 (Mark 6:34-44), so the compassion of Jesus moved Him to feed this second crowd.

Ask someone to read the introductory paragraphs prior to asking a few other group members to read sections of Mark 8:1-10. After reading the passage, respond to the following questions.

❑ **What does Jesus' compassion allow Him to see?** (E.g., the people's physical need for food; their hunger; their tiredness; their inability to travel back home if they didn't eat.)

LEADER'S GUIDE

NOTE: The word *compassion* is translated from the Greek word *splanchnizomai*. It is used in Matthew, Mark, and Luke to refer to the attitude of Jesus and actions of persons in three parables: the Unforgiving Servant (Matthew 18:23-35); the Prodigal Son (Luke 15:11-32); and the Good Samaritan (Luke 10:30-37). It means to have pity, show mercy, feel sympathy. It is derived from *splanchna*, meaning inward parts, which refers to the seat of the emotion, the heart. The expression of sympathy or empathy, "my heart goes out to you," reflects the sense of compassion to which we are referring. One may actually experience a physical as well as emotional response to the sight or knowledge of human need.

According to the *New International Dictionary of New Testament Theology* (vol. 2, p. 600), *splanchnizomai* makes the unbounded mercy of God visible and expresses "the attitude of complete willingness to use all means, time, strength, and life, for saving at the crucial moment.... Humanity and neighborliness [as in the story of the Good Samaritan] are not qualities but action."

❏ **What objection do the disciples raise to feeding the people?** (E.g., the need is too great; there's nowhere to get the food; there isn't enough food; there are too many people; they are in a remote area.)

❏ **What excuses do you tend to use when trying to avoid meeting a need you see in the world? List some of the "I don't have enough..." statements you use.** (E.g., I don't have enough time; I don't have enough courage; I don't have enough faith; I don't have enough money; I don't have enough people to help; I don't have enough love or compassion; I don't have enough knowledge or information; I don't have enough power or influence; etc.)

❏ **What did Jesus do when the disciples offered Him the food they had?** (He took the seven loaves of bread, gave thanks, broke them, and gave them back to the disciples to set before the people. He did the same with a few small fish.)

❏ **What were the explicit and implicit outcomes of the feeding of the 4,000?** (Verse 8 explicitly states: "The

DARE TO RISK

people ate and were satisfied." Implicit outcomes include: The people's need was met; they experienced the compassion and love of Jesus; the power of God was made manifest; the people experienced a miracle; the faith of the disciples grew; perhaps more people began to follow Jesus.)

❑ **What are some lessons you can glean from this story?** (We need to offer what we have to God, no matter how small it seems, to be used for His purposes in meeting the needs of the world. When we offer what we have to God, whatever it is, He blesses it and we may see a multiplication of resources. We need to look beyond our human limitations to see the limitless provision and power of God. Compassion moves one to action. Apparent inability to meet a need should not dictate a no-action response to it. Jesus doesn't only minister directly to needy people Himself, but He uses disciples who make themselves and their resources available to meet the needs of others.)

As you discuss the last two questions, encourage group members to share how they will specifically apply the lessons learned in this story.

Optional — Rebuilding the Wall
The story of Nehemiah takes place after the Jews have returned from exile in Babylon. It is about a man who led the Jews to rebuild the walls of Jerusalem after they had been destroyed. He had a vision, a plan, and was able to mobilize the people so that they accomplished the task in 52 days.

It was not an easy task, however. Nehemiah experienced resistance from Sanballat, governor of Samaria, the primary political adversary of Nehemiah, and resistance at times from the Jews themselves. They got discouraged at the enormity of the rebuilding task and distracted by opposition from others.

Divide into six smaller groups to outline Nehemiah 1–6. Assign one chapter per group. Ask each group to outline or summarize the chapter they have been given. If your total group size is fairly small, you may have a few persons working alone.

Pocket Principle

1 When you focus on Scripture in your lesson, be sure to have a concordance, Bible dictionary and, if appropriate, a commentary handy for reference. Often a question regarding culture or history will come up in the course of a discussion which can be quickly answered if these texts are readily available. If the question asked doesn't demand immediate attention before the discussion can continue, ask someone to look up the answer for you so that you can continue facilitating the discussion until the answer is found. This way, the group doesn't have to wait for you and you get others involved in the teaching process.

Give at least 7–10 minutes for people to complete this assignment. Then go chapter by chapter, asking groups/persons to give a summary of important things that happened in the chapter they studied, giving special attention to Nehemiah as a risk-taker, man of conviction, and advocate for social justice and the welfare of his people. If a significant point is omitted as people report on their chapters, make sure to mention it before moving on to the next chapter.

Pocket Principle

2 When leading a discussion which involves addressing a number of questions, do not always ask if anyone else has something to say or wait until there is silence before moving to the next question. If you do, the discussion tends to lose momentum and drag. By moving the discussion along, you do run the risk of missing a few comments, but you can give people opportunity at the end of the discussion for any final remarks.

DARE TO RISK

When everyone has a sense of the story line and of Nehemiah as a repairer of broken walls, lead a discussion using the following questions:

❏ **What do you think enabled Nehemiah to even think about rebuilding the walls of Jerusalem?** (Compassion for the people and love for the city; a close relationship with God; willingness to be available for God's purposes; willingness to take risks; confidence in who God is; etc.)

❏ **What do you think enabled Nehemiah to keep going in the midst of such adversity and opposition?** (He was a person of prayer; he had faith; he believed in God's power; he could picture the wall rebuilt; he didn't let the opposition get to him; he looked more at God than at the rubble; he was able to remain single-minded; etc.)

❏ **In what ways did Nehemiah work for the justice and the welfare of his people?** (By rebuilding the walls the people would possess greater security and protection. He confronted the nobles and officials about their wrongdoing and abusive monetary practices [chap. 5]. He prayed for and identified with the people. He mobilized them and gave them hope and good work to do [2:17-18].)

❏ **How does Nehemiah show us that one person can make a difference in the world?** (He made changes for the better: the wall got built; abusive monetary practices were stopped; people were put to productive work; he turned them to God; etc.)

❏ **What is God personally telling you through the lives and examples of risk-takers like Nehemiah and Peter?** (Make sure individuals share what God is telling them personally through the stories of Nehemiah and Peter.)

GROWING BY DOING   15–20 minutes

Ready, Set, Go!
Guide the group through a session of brainstorming. Explain how to brainstorm and help them to engage in the process.

Pocket Principle

3 Brainstorming is a useful group technique when you want people to generate a variety of ideas. When you use it, be sure to explain that in the initial stages no one is to judge another person's idea. No idea is to be considered far-fetched. In this way, people are given permission to use their imaginations and offer suggestions without fear that their suggestions will be considered silly or inappropriate.

Encourage people to not only think of things to do as a one-time activity, but also discuss ways they could be involved long-term (e.g., prison visitation, soup kitchen work, halfway house counseling, hospital visitation, literacy projects, tutoring, Habitat for Humanity, Meals on Wheels, clothing and food distribution, etc.). After several ideas have been suggested, help the group to narrow down the possibilities to one in which the entire group can participate. Then ask for one or two volunteers to be responsible for planning and coordinating the activity for the group.

Pocket Principle

4 As your group becomes more comfortable with each other, it is important for you as a leader to find ways for group members to begin taking on more leadership responsibility and ownership of the group. This not only frees up your time, but gives others opportunity to use their gifts and abilities, develop leadership skills, and serve the other members.

Close by praying over the project and the needs of the community and world that were identified in your brainstorming.

Optional–Change Our Hearts, Move Our Feet
Confession and repentance are key to changed hearts and lives. Prayer opens us up to feel the things that break the heart of God. In prayer, the Spirit floods us with compassion

DARE TO RISK

as well as conviction. Our response to the poor is the outcome of a heart in tune with God's heart.

If your group would benefit most from an extended time of prayer, you may want to use this option. Explain clearly the reason for the prayer time and the nature of conversational prayer, if people are unfamiliar with it. Tell them that the group will start with silent prayer and then move into conversational prayer. Lead by opening up the time of silence with a beginning prayer; then after several minutes pray again to open up the time for conversational prayer. Close the time when everyone who has felt led to pray aloud has done so.

Be sure to give the group ample opportunity to confess their sins, express their feelings and concerns before God, and give Him the opportunity to minister, forgive, heal, and empower. You may want to frame the entire time with a Scripture reference such as 2 Chronicles 7:14: "If My people, who are called by My name, will humble themselves and pray and seek My face and turn from their wicked ways, then will I hear from heaven and will forgive their sin and will heal their land."

After your time of prayer together, allow group members to share what they experienced, including what the Lord revealed to them in prayer.

GOING THE SECOND MILE   5 minutes

Encourage group members to pray about the "loaves" God is asking them to offer Him and to think about how God might want them to use those "loaves" in meeting specific needs in the community and world. Answer any questions people might have about the information they are to collect. If you want the data to be standardized, you may wish to develop a form which each person can fill out. Doing so would make it much easier to compile a resource guide or directory for the group or your church.

Optional—Follow the Leader
Hebrews 13:7 reads:

> ⁷**Remember your leaders, who spoke the Word of God to you. Consider the outcome of their way of life and imitate their faith.**

Christians have much to learn from others who demonstrate how to live out one's convictions. Encourage group members to gather information and write up a biographical sketch of one such person. Examples include Martin Luther King, Jr., Mother Teresa, Dorothy Day, John Howard Yoder, and Amy Carmichael.

GROWING AS A LEADER

The Pocket Principles given in sessions 4 and 5 are intended to help you in your communications skills as a small group leader. How well did you practice the following skills during this session?

- ❏ Paraphrasing: During a discussion or in an informal conversation, when did I seek to get at the meaning and feelings of a person by trying to restate what I heard? How often did I use such phrases as, "You seem to be saying...," or "I sense you're feeling..."?

- ❏ Opinion-seeking/information-seeking: How aware was I of people who were not contributing to the discussion? Did I ever ask questions to draw people into the discussion or conversation? How did I do it?

- ❏ Opinion ownership: Was I aware of anyone using generalities rather than owning their statements or opinions? What did I do about it? To what extent did I model responses that shared my own personal feelings?

- ❏ Which communication skills do I find difficult to practice, and what will I do to improve?

SEVEN

Staying Afloat with God

It's one thing to choose to take a risk in order to be obedient to God. It's another to be able to live with the consequences of that choice when those consequences involve major obstacles, frustrations, fears, and doubts. Once out of the boat, our ability to walk toward Jesus on the water depends on how well we are able to keep our eyes fixed on Him, not the "waves" we encounter.

Our ability to keep our eyes "fixed" has to do with developing and caring for our relationship with God. This is the relationship that not only motivates us to get out of the boat but sustains us on the water. Only as we become more intimate with Him can we continue to trust and depend on Him, walking by faith in all things.

One of the ways Jesus maintained a vital relationship with God while He was on earth was through the spiritual discipline of solitude. He was able to keep obedient to the will and work of His Father in heaven by spending quality time alone with Him. In a similar way, solitude is one of God's ways to help us to maintain unbroken eye contact with Jesus as we walk on water.

If you as a leader are unfamiliar with the discipline of solitude, Richard Foster's book *Celebration of Discipline* has help-

LEADER'S GUIDE

ful chapters on both solitude and meditation. Explain to the group that this session is only an introduction to the discipline. The focus is on understanding its importance with reference to risk-taking. Solitude helps us to get to know God better. And the better we know God, the more we'll be able to risk in obedience; we'll be able to trust Him to take care of us as we risk because of the intimate relationship we share with Him.

As group leader, you have the option to select which elements best fit your group, your style of leadership, and your purposes. After you examine the Session Objectives, choose the activities that seem the most appropriate for your group.

SESSION OBJECTIVES

✓ To recognize that being able to "stay afloat" as we live out our risk-taking has to do with keeping our eyes fixed on Jesus.
✓ To identify activities that help maintain a growing relationship with God.
✓ To examine Jesus' practice of the discipline of solitude and its use in His life and ministry.
✓ To increase commitment to the practice of the discipline of solitude as a way to help us keep fellowship with God, and to begin to practice it more consistently.

GETTING ACQUAINTED   15–20 minutes

As group members arrive, collect the information sheets they compiled as part of last session's Going the Second Mile. When everyone is present, begin this week's session by asking someone to read The Other Half of the Story. Then work through Up Close and Personal together.

Up Close and Personal
The purpose of this exercise to help people to see that intimate relationships are based on such things as quality time together, trust, and love. Ask each person to think of someone with

123

whom he or she has a very close relationship. Then ask people to describe the characteristics of the relationship, including how they became so intimate with the other person (e.g., trust, honesty, vulnerability, unconditional love, time together, crises, praying together, etc.). After soliciting responses, ask: How does your relationship with the other person get you through the difficult times in life? Then ask: How is your relationship with God similar or different from your relationship with this person? Finally ask: What things do you do personally to develop a closer relationship with God? The purpose of this question is to help group members begin thinking about how intentional they are in developing their relationship with God and to identify the various ways people seek to get to know God better.

GAINING INSIGHT   30–35 minutes

Experiencing Solitude

Introduce this section by reading or asking someone to read the first paragraph in it. Then lead group members through the mini-experience of solitude as a way to move them into the Scripture study.

Tell everyone that for the next 10 minutes they will be given the opportunity to spend time alone with God. They are not to read their Bibles, talk to each other, or do anything but sit in His presence. Direct them to various parts of the house or building so that they are as separated from each other as possible. Tell them that you will call them back together after the time is up.

Pocket Principle

1 Whenever you break up the larger group into smaller units or ask people to move themselves physically in some way, more time is involved in dispersing and regathering them than you think. For a group of 8 to 12, if an activity requires moving people and chairs around, add about 5 to 7 minutes to the total amount of time allotted for the actual activity.

After the designated time, regather the group. Debrief their experience with the following questions:

❏ **What feelings did you experience during your time alone with God?** (I couldn't concentrate; I got bored; I really enjoyed it; I didn't know what to do with myself; I felt close to God; etc.)

❏ **Other than your daily devotional times, what intentional or extended periods of time have you experienced being alone with God? How have they affected your relationship with God?** (Retreats, conferences, walks alone, on vacation, etc. These times have enabled my relationship with God to grow; they've made me feel closer to Him; I depend on Him and trust Him more; they've made me feel more distant from Him because I don't seem to get anything out of the time; etc.)

Read the material which follows the questions. Ask for any feedback or thoughts before moving on.

Optional—Fixed or Out of Focus?
This exercise is good if a number of your group members have already chosen to take risks in faith and obedience. They can then share from their own experience their responses to this question: What are the things that distract you from keeping your eyes fixed on Jesus as you walk in faith, and what kinds of things help you to keep focused?

Retreating to Move Ahead
Ask someone to read the Introduction to this section. Ask a second person to read Mark 1:35-39. Then facilitate a discussion using the questions in the student book.

Pocket Principle

2 If the Scripture passage for your meeting or any other part of the lesson you are leading is unfamiliar to you, spend time beforehand gaining more knowledge and information about it. This not only enhances your own growth but also benefits the entire group as you share what you have learned through your individual study. However, if after seeking to learn more, you still feel uncomfortable with the material, try to find someone who can help you or teach that portion for you.

☐ **What do you observe about Jesus' practice of the discipline of solitude?** (He did it very early in the morning [still dark]; He didn't stay in bed but got up and left the house; He went to a deserted place; once there, He prayed.)

☐ **What kinds of principles might you draw about the discipline of solitude, given verse 35?** (1. A good time for solitude may be very early in the morning or when there's little activity around you. 2. The place should be away from usual surroundings. 3. The place should be quiet, with no distractions. 4. Prayer is the primary content of solitude, listening and speaking with God.)

NOTE: While the example of Jesus in the Mark passage points to prayer as central to solitude, be sure to communicate that solitude can have other aspects to it, such as silence, worship, meditation, Bible reading, listening to praise tapes, and journaling. Encourage group members to discover more about solitude on their own.

Pocket Principle

3 Helping people to go from observation to application is key in making sure they personalize what they learn. Slow down and take more time to interact if people are having trouble understanding how a passage or principle of Scripture applies to their lives.

☐ **What did Jesus tell His companions after they found Him? Then what did He do?** (He told them that they were all going to the neighboring towns so that He could proclaim the Gospel. Then He went throughout Galilee proclaiming the message and casting out demons.)

LEADER'S GUIDE

❑ **Given what is recorded in verses 38 and 39, what do you think was the outcome of Jesus' time of solitude with God?** (Guidance from God; empowerment for ministry; fellowship with the Father; resistance to temptation; motivation and increased confidence, etc.)

Ask people to read out loud the material after the questions, one person per paragraph. After going through it, ask if group members have any questions, comments, or feedback they want to share. Be sure to help people make the connection between the fruit of solitude and the ability to take risks in faith and obedience.

GROWING BY DOING   20–25 minutes

NOTE: This activity will be most helpful and practical to the group if you are able to give them a list of suggestions for places in your area to retreat for solitude. These may include retreat centers, conference grounds, Christian campuses, and prayer chapels. Your pastor, Catholic churches in your area, or Christian schools and seminaries may all have lists to give you. If group members have such a list, they will find it much easier to expose themselves to and practice the discipline of solitude.

As you work through the Growing by Doing exercise, give people opportunity to spend a few minutes individually thinking through how they can begin to practice the discipline of solitude in their own lives. Ask them to write down the possibilities and then commit to one thing they will do during the coming week. It may be to take part of a weekend and go away alone to be with God or to use an hour lunch break to drive to a quiet park to spend time with the Lord. Some people may commit to calling around to the various retreat centers near their home to find one they can begin frequenting monthly.

After 10 minutes, ask people to get into pairs to share how they want to hold each other accountable to the things they decided to do to make solitude a part of their lives the following week. Encourage them to pray for each other after they finish sharing their action plans.

DARE TO RISK

GOING THE SECOND MILE — 5 minutes

Ask group members to come prepared next time to share what they experienced with reference to solitude, however they incorporated it into their lives that week. As part of their processing of their experience, ask them to write down a response to the two questions given.

GROWING AS A LEADER

Solitude in Leadership

Thomas Merton once wrote: "We do not go into the desert to escape people but to learn how to find them; we do not leave them in order to have nothing more to do with them, but to find out the way to do them the most good" (*New Seeds of Contemplation,* New Directions, 1961, p. 80). Henri Nouwen adds, "Compassion is the fruit of all solitude and the basis of all ministry. The purification and transformation that take place in solitude manifest themselves in compassion" (*The Way of the Heart,* Ballantine Books, 1981, p. 20).

Being a leader in small group ministry requires compassion for others and discovery of "the way to do them the most good." We are called to be involved in God's work of transforming their lives, not simply informing their heads. And if solitude helps us to do that, then we need to ask ourselves these kinds of questions:

❑ How do I personally see the relationship between solitude and my leadership ability?

❑ To what extent have I experienced the fruit of solitude, and to what extent can that fruit be seen in my life?

Compassion: How has time alone with God given me compassion for others? How does it show itself in the small group?

Perspective: In what ways has my perspective about the small group changed since session 1? How have I been able to refocus on Jesus or gain God's perspective on the group and my part as a result of time alone with God?

LEADER'S GUIDE

Refreshment: How refreshed or burned out do I feel this seventh session of our small group? How has my time alone with God or lack of it been a factor in how I feel?

Empowerment for ministry: How empowered for ministry have I felt as I have led this group? What evidence has there been of that power? How has spending time or not spending time in solitude been a factor?

❑ Are there any changes I need to make in how I practice the discipline of solitude? What are they, and what will I do?

❑ How can I encourage others to pursue the discipline?

EIGHT

Staying Afloat with the Community of Faith

When God calls us to Himself, He also calls us into community. Discipleship was never meant to be a solitary journey. We need both solitude and community to grow in our relationship with God through Jesus Christ. And, as Richard Foster states, we must cultivate both if we are to live in obedience (*Celebration of Discipline,* p. 98).

From personal experience we know the value and importance of people who stand by us, encourage us, exhort us, admonish us, affirm us, pray for us. God doesn't intend for us to "go it alone," and it is an especially foolish thing to do when we are trying to take risks in faith and obedience. Unless we have water walkers with us, we will surely have a more difficult time staying afloat. Do you think Peter would have gotten distracted so easily by the wind and the waves if Andrew, his brother, had also gotten out of the boat with him?

This last session looks at the role of the Christian community in risk-taking and helps your group members put closure on your time together. As group leader, you have the option to select which elements best fit your group, your style of leadership, and your purposes. After you examine the Session Objectives, choose the activities that seem most appropriate for your group.

LEADER'S GUIDE

> **SESSION OBJECTIVES**
>
> ✓ To understand the necessity to be in fellowship with other water walkers.
> ✓ To determine how to continue to support one another in risk-taking.
> ✓ To affirm one another and our efforts to become more obedient to God.
> ✓ To celebrate what God has done in and through the small group.

GETTING ACQUAINTED   10–15 minutes
Pocket Principle

1 In any last session of a small group experience, it is important to end on a positive note. Seek to make the meeting celebrative. Add flowers or a special cake with the names of the group members written on it. Be upbeat but sensitive to the sadness that comes with closure.

Ask a few people to share what they experienced in the area of solitude since the last session. Discuss the kind of impact it made on their lives. Then ask someone to read Cocooning or Community?

Solo and Several
This activity provides an introduction to the topic of Christian community and draws on people's perceptions and experiences with it. Ask someone to read the material in this section, and then lead the group in a discussion using these questions:

❑ **What does the phrase "Christian community" mean to you?** (E.g., the church; a tightly knit fellowship of believers in Jesus Christ; koinonia; a group of Christians who support and care for each other; love and unity in the Spirit; etc.)

131

DARE TO RISK

❏ **When have you experienced Christian community, and what was it like?** (E.g., I experience it in this small group; I feel it when I worship on Sundays; I sense it when I gather together to pray with others; etc.)

Optional—Strength in Numbers
Ask one group member to do something which would be made easier if others helped him or her. For example, ask the person to move a large table or other piece of furniture without assistance. Then when the person is unable to or finds the task difficult to do, ask these questions:

❏ **What point or principle does this object lesson illustrate to you?**

❏ **When in your own experience as a Christian did you find something easier to do when you had the help or encouragement of other believers?**

After the discussion, read the first two paragraphs under Solo and Several as a way to introduce Characteristics of Community.

Pocket Principle

2 Very often the leader is perceived as having all the answers. To avoid this perception, redirect a question you're asked by throwing it open to the group. This way, you don't answer all the questions, and you give others opportunity to contribute.

GAINING INSIGHT   35–40 minutes

Characteristics of Community
This activity examines the characteristics of Christian community as they are laid out by the Apostle Paul in his letter to the Colossians. Read the passage together and discuss the following questions:

❏ **Who makes up the Christian community, and what does it mean to be holy and dearly loved?** (We're God's chosen ones. We're "set apart" for His service;

LEADER'S GUIDE

we're made holy by His grace, by His decision; we are loved by God.)

❑ **What qualities are God's "chosen people" to demonstrate, and why do you think these are so important in Christian community?** (Compassion, kindness, humility, gentleness, and patience. These are important because they affect the quality of our relationships with one another. They are all relational characteristics whose opposites bring about such things as division, factions, strife, envy, cruelty, anger, and mistreatment.)

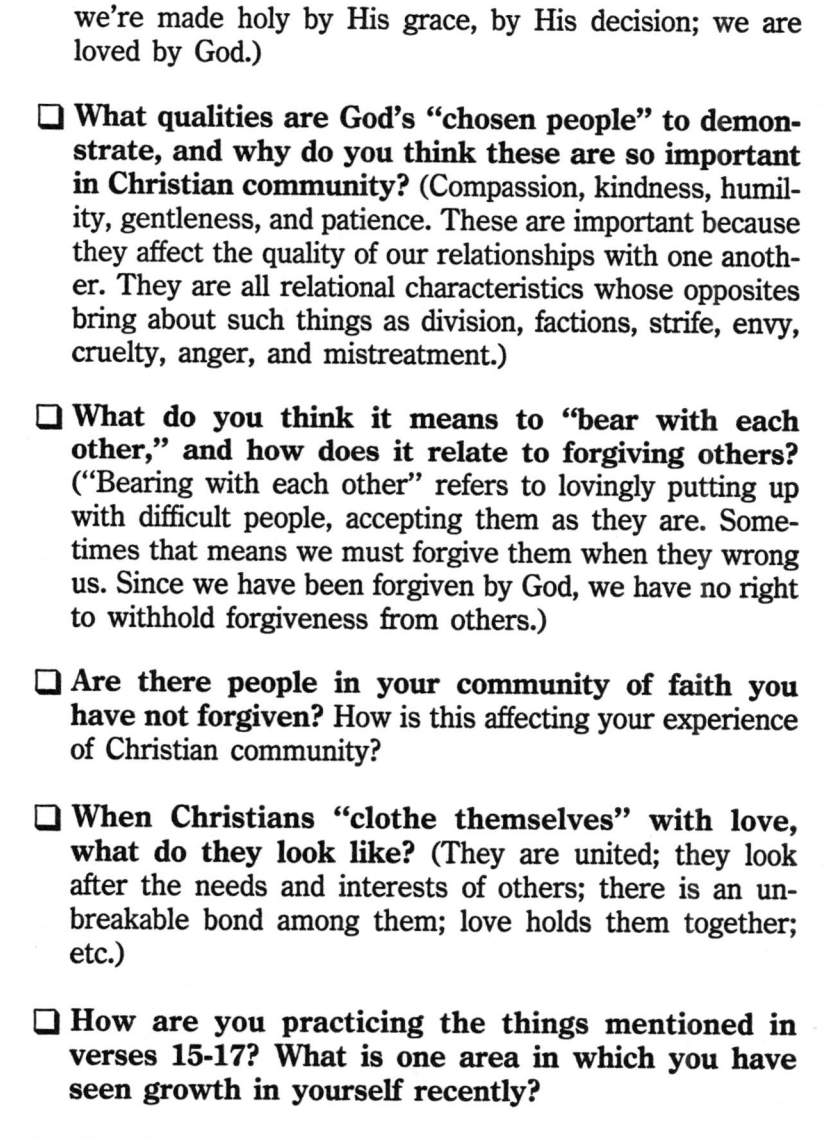

❑ **What do you think it means to "bear with each other," and how does it relate to forgiving others?** ("Bearing with each other" refers to lovingly putting up with difficult people, accepting them as they are. Sometimes that means we must forgive them when they wrong us. Since we have been forgiven by God, we have no right to withhold forgiveness from others.)

❑ **Are there people in your community of faith you have not forgiven?** How is this affecting your experience of Christian community?

❑ **When Christians "clothe themselves" with love, what do they look like?** (They are united; they look after the needs and interests of others; there is an unbreakable bond among them; love holds them together; etc.)

❑ **How are you practicing the things mentioned in verses 15-17? What is one area in which you have seen growth in yourself recently?**

Pocket Principle

3 As the leader, usually your comments and words carry more weight than those of others. For this last session, in particular, be sure to take time to affirm and encourage each person before the meeting is over. People will tend to remember what you share with them, so choose your

DARE TO RISK

thoughts carefully. Make the time to pray and prepare beforehand.

The following two exercises are meant to help people articulate how the small group has made a difference in their lives and to give them opportunity to affirm and thank one another as the group experience draws to a close.

Koinonia
Ask the group to respond to the questions and material presented in this section.

Pocket Principle

4 When discussing a question in which personal application or disclosure is asked for, be sensitive to the tone of the responses given. If some people show signs of getting emotional (their voices start to quiver, they begin crying or fidgeting in their chairs), give them time to regain their composure. After a few moments of silence, sometimes it is helpful to ask if they would like the group to pray for them right then and there. By asking, you let them decide, and they can tell you what is most helpful to them.

Two Are Better Than One
Ask someone to read Ecclesiastes 4:9-10, then discuss the two questions.

GROWING BY DOING   15–20 minutes

Passing the Blessing
Affirmation and prayer are two important aspects of Christian community, and in the final meeting it is important to make them a part of the experience of closure. Ask someone to read Passing the Blessing, then instruct them on how the group will bless one another.

Before the meeting begins, write each person's name on a slip of paper. Fold the papers in half and put them in a small bowl or basket. During the time of blessing, pass around the container and tell each person to take one of the slips of paper. Tell them that they are to give a blessing to the person whose name they have drawn. The blessing should include what they appreciate about the person and the kind of future in risk-taking they envision for him or her (e.g., "I appreciate your honesty and vulnerability, and I see you taking more and more risks in obedience as you witness at work."). Give group members one or two minutes to think about their blessings before beginning.

After everyone has shared blessings with each other, join hands and spend time in conversational prayer, thanking God for the persons in the group and what He has done in your midst as a community of faith.

GOING THE SECOND MILE   5–10 minutes

What's Next?
Ask someone to read Hebrews 10:24-25. Then briefly discuss if there is a "next step" for the group or what the next step should be for individuals. Give group members opportunity to set up a future meeting time if they want to continue to meet socially or as a small group. Be prepared to respond to questions about your willingness to continue as the leader.

Offer any parting words to the group, encouraging them to continue taking risks and seeking to be obedient to God. Then end the meeting and the series with a closing prayer.

Optional—Reunion!
Set a date about a month after the last meeting for a potluck dinner, picnic, or fun outing in which family and friends can also participate. This will ensure a formal time of touching base and continuing to encourage one another. You may ask group members to be prepared to give testimonies about what God has done in their lives since the last meeting as they continue to take risks in faith and obedience to Him.

DARE TO RISK

GROWING AS A LEADER

Personal Assessment
Take some time to reflect on your role as the leader of this small group and what you experienced:

❑ Looking back, to what extent was leading this group an actual risk-taking experience for you, and how did you see God keeping you afloat?

❑ To what extent were your expectations fulfilled for the group?

❑ In what areas did you see yourself develop as a leader over the course of the eight sessions (e.g., communication skills, vulnerability, acceptance, use of humor, etc.)?

❑ What will you do next with the leadership skills you have developed in this group?